EDUCATION IN MODERN SOCIETY

ORGANISATION FOR ECONOMIC CO-OPERATION AND DEVELOPMENT

Pursuant to article 1 of the Convention signed in Paris on 14th December, 1960, and which came into force on 30th September, 1961, the Organisation for Economic Co-operation and Development (OECD) shall promote policies designed:

- to achieve the highest sustainable economic growth and employment and a rising standard of living in Member countries, while maintaining financial stability, and thus to contribute to the development of the world economy;
- to contribute to sound economic expansion in Member as well as non-member countries in the process of economic development; and
- to contribute to the expansion of world trade on a multilateral, non-discriminatory basis in accordance with international obligations.

The Signatories of the Convention on the OECD are Austria, Belgium, Canada, Denmark, France, the Federal Republic of Germany, Greece, Iceland, Ireland, Italy, Luxembourg, the Netherlands, Norway, Portugal, Spain, Sweden, Switzerland, Turkey, the United Kingdom and the United States. The following countries acceded subsequently to this Convention (the dates are those on which the instruments of accession were deposited): Japan (28th April, 1964), Finland (28th January, 1969), Australia (7th June, 1971) and New Zealand (29th May, 1973).

The Socialist Federal Republic of Yugoslavia takes part in certain work of the OECD (agreement of 28th October, 1961).

Publié en français sous le titre:

L'ENSEIGNEMENT
DANS LA SOCIÉTÉ MODERNE

The distinctive perspective applied by the OECD to its educational activities derives from the importance attached to the interaction between education, the economy and the wider society. At no time has this perspective been more appropriate than in the current decade as OECD countries experience rapid social, cultural, economic and technological change. These changes, and their manifold implications for education and training, are discussed in this report.

Placed in the context of the issues that inform the contemporary debate as well as the measured trends in student numbers, educational expenditures and institutional structures, the report examines the major features of education's changing socio-economic environment. These include structural changes in employment and the labour market, the outstanding problem of unemployment, shorter working time, and rapid technological development. No less important are the social and cultural aspects of current change and the report gives particular emphasis to the position of the socially disadvantaged, cultural minorities and migrants, and women, as well as discussing the family, the community, and values in education.

The more general socio-economic issues are complemented by the specific questions that arise in each of the main sectors of the education systems of OECD countries, and compulsory schooling, post-compulsory education and training, and higher education are considered in turn. Dominant themes include the importance of improving the quality of schooling, the low-achievement problem, bridging the divide between education and training, opening more widely education's doors to adults, and maintaining and protecting research capacity. Questions of expenditure and finance, crucial to the implementation of educational policies, are separately identified and an overview of the report and its conclusions are contained in the final chapter.

The main author of the report is David Istance of the Education and Training Division in the Directorate for Social Affairs, Manpower and Education drawing substantially in some chapters upon contributions from his colleagues and upon recent OECD reports covering the same subjects in depth. It was prepared for the meeting at Ministerial level of the OECD Education Committee on the 20th-21st November 1984 and published on the responsibility of the Secretary-General.

3

Also available

EDUCATIONAL TRENDS IN THE 1970s. A Quantitative Analysis (November 1984)
(91 84 02 1) ISBN 92-64-12630-9   146 pages   £6.00   US$12.00   F60.00

INDUSTRY AND UNIVERSITY. New Forms of Co-operation and Communication (October 1984)
(92 84 04 1) ISBN 92-64-12607-4   70 pages
£3.50   US$7.00   F35.00

EDUCATION, URBAN DEVELOPMENT AND LOCAL INITIATIVES (February 1984)
(96 84 01 1) ISBN 92-64-12536-1   110 pages
£6.00   US$12.00   F60.00

EDUCATIONAL PLANNING. A Reappraisal (December 1983)
(91 83 05 1) ISBN 92-64-12500-0   360 pages
£12.00   US$24.00   F120.00

POLICIES FOR HIGHER EDUCATION IN THE 1980s. Intergovernmental Conference, OECD, 12th-14th October 1981 (July 1983)
(91 83 03 1) ISBN 92-64-12448-9   234 pages
£9.50   US$19.00   F95.00

EDUCATION AND WORK. The Views of the Young (July 1983)
(96 83 02 1) ISBN 92-64-12464-0   122 pages
£4.80   US$9.75   F48.00

THE EDUCATION OF THE HANDICAPPED ADOLESCENT:

THE TRANSITION FROM SCHOOL TO WORKING LIFE (July 1983)
(96 83 01 1) ISBN 92-64-12438-1   192 pages
£7.40   US$15.00   F74.00

INTEGRATION IN THE SCHOOL (August 1981)
(96 81 02 1) ISBN 92-64-12229-X   150 pages
£3.80   US$8.50   F38.00

COMPULSORY SCHOOLING IN A CHANGING WORLD (April 1983)
(91 83 02 1) ISBN 92-64-12430-6   150 pages
£8.50   US$17.00   F85.00

To be published in 1985:
NEW POLICIES FOR THE YOUNG

EDUCATION AND TRAINING AFTER BASIC SCHOOLING

Prices charged at the OECD Publications Office.

*THE OECD CATALOGUE OF PUBLICATIONS and supplements will be sent free of charge
on request addressed either to OECD Publications Office,
2, rue André-Pascal, 75775 PARIS CEDEX 16, or to the OECD Sales Agent in your country.*

TABLE OF CONTENTS

Part One

THE CONTEXT AND SITUATION
OF EDUCATION TODAY

Chapter 1

THE NEW CONTEXT OF THE DEBATE ON EDUCATION

INTRODUCTION

Education is a vast and complex enterprise, and one that absorbs very large amounts of public as well as private resources. It takes place in a myriad of schools, colleges and other institutions that make up the highly organised education systems of OECD countries. The demand for knowledge ever grows as society and all groups within it appreciate its centrality to modern life. With the technological developments of the latter decades organised learning and complex knowledge can theoretically be acquired without stepping into a classroom or directly confronting a teacher. Education takes place in a multitude of non-formal settings, many outside the direct control of educational administrations.

While education can and must be understood in terms of its own aims, functions and special missions, it does not stand in isolation from the wider society around it. It is constantly influenced and moulded by the forces of cultural, social, economic and political change. It is linked in a complex way to the process of economic and social development and carries the heavy responsibility to contribute to that development. The overall examination of education cannot but take place against this background, and yet it cannot be subordinated to it.

This report seeks to examine the wide-ranging current developments within education and the issues and questions confronting the main sectors of education systems today in relation to this wider context. What are the principal features of these economic, technological, social and cultural worlds that education must also contribute and respond to? Such a focus is necessarily long-term: without neglecting the immediate problems that confront education, the perspective extends well beyond the short term. An issue that recurs throughout the chapters that follow is precisely the need to find a more satisfactory balance between considerations of the immediate and the longer term.

The report begins with a succinct presentation of some of the basic facts of education today, encompassing the socio-economic as well as the more strictly educational. Part Two – The Socio-Economic Environment of Education – examines economic, social, and cultural questions and developments (Chapters 3, 4 and 5) and seeks to identify some of the broad implications for education. In Part Three – Educational Responses in the Eighties – the sectors of compulsory, post-compulsory secondary, and higher education are the subjects of the subsequent three chapters, including, in Chapter 9, a discussion of questions relating specifically to the financing of education. Part Four draws together the main themes and conclusions.

CONTINUITY AND CHANGE IN EDUCATIONAL DEBATE AND POLICY-MAKING

Obsession with change often results in neglect of the continuity that permeates the policy aspirations and functioning of education systems. Lack of change is frequently presented in terms of impediments to the constant improvement of the institutions that provide education. Much of educational policy, however, concerns trade-offs that improve one element only at the expense of another. The degree to which change has taken place and should be realised must not, therefore, be exaggerated. The main goals and aspirations of policy inherited from recent decades remain essentially valid and inspire this report, even if their interpretation and the more specific priorities alter with time. For education systems to be in a state of constant, rapid flux is no more desirable than that they should be totally static, impervious to change in the world around them. And one important fact that has not changed is that education is just as central now to the social and economic fabric of OECD countries as before, a position established on the basis of the confidence and expansion of the post-war years.

But change there certainly has been, in some cases, rapid. Dominating features behind this change have been large-scale demographic fluctuations, economic recession and its impact upon public expenditures, high levels of unemployment particularly of young people, rapid technological and structural change, and evolving social and political attitudes and aspirations. Apart from more measurable aspects of change such as those of educational resource levels, student numbers and choices, and institutional growth or decline, an equally important qualitative change is the increased questioning apparent in many places concerning the present organisation and benefits of education. Levels of current criticism are unprecedented: do schools and colleges achieve their basic missions? Do they give value for the large sums of public money devoted to them?

This change is made more apparent through contrast with the seemingly euphoric years of the 1960s and early 1970s. Then, in a context of economic growth and full employment, ever more ambitious goals and expectations were set for education. School populations grew very rapidly and larger shares of public wealth were made available to sustain educational expansion. Yet interpreting the present situation in terms of this contrast can be misleading. It is highly likely that greater public scrutiny of education would have taken place irrespective of the economic reversals of the 1970s, with the need to assess the impact of the wide-ranging structural reforms and the degree to which the ambitious goals were met. The contrast would also be misleading if the focus were exclusively upon education, to the degree that the whole array of policies and programmes that comprise the Welfare State are now under closer scrutiny. The notion of a "crisis" of the Welfare State, particularly in the financial means to sustain it, has acquired greater currency. Yet as economic recovery takes hold, it becomes apparent that finance is not the whole of the matter and that the rightful role of the public authorities, the place of State provision and alternatives to it, are becoming the subject of serious policy debate. In other words, the pertinent changes have by no means been experienced by education alone, and it is more than a question of the availability of financial resources.

Greater criticism of education and the general questioning of provision not only derive from economic forces and political pressures to reverse certain of the policy trends of recent decades. An understanding of the present context of educational debate must also fully recognise the extent to which a variety of social groups and sections of the population seek a greater share of the benefits of education. This means having greater access to available provision but it also means having a larger say in the making of educational policy both in

10

terms of the determination of priorities and in the shaping of the actual content of education itself. Pressures to extend the role of the community are an expression of this as are the more specific examples of women or cultural and racial minorities demanding a more equitable reflection of their interests. And, more broadly, there is an underlying questioning of the ways and means of achieving equality of opportunity – to what extent is there a conflict between egalitarianism and excellence?

Together, these changes have meant that the educational debate has become increasingly politicised and interests that traditionally have been regarded as external to education intervene in decision-making and control to a greater extent. The sharpening of competition to enjoy the benefits of education following the curtailment of resource growth, and the widened claims for a voice in policy-making, imply that a general consensus can no longer be assumed. The politicisation of education brings questions of power, and therefore of conflict, to the fore. Debate has thus become more complex, and the role of educational policy-makers is rendered especially problematic. They have not only to confront a world of troubling economic and social change where there can be less reliance upon general consensus; but education now extends well beyond their ambit, and other groups, interests, and administrations are intimately involved in the making of educational policy.

Yet, perhaps paradoxically, the expectations held out for, and challenges facing, education have never been greater. Demand for education grows. Economic and social change have increased, not diminished, the need for a substantial educational response. The essentially moral – and certainly ambitious – objective that each child should be educated to the limits of her or his ability appears to have survived the economic thunder. The nature of the challenges and changes confronting education is elaborated in the following chapters, the underlying reality being that education's role and responsibility in the modern world has never been more critical.

Chapter 2

EDUCATION TODAY: SOME BASIC FACTS[1]

GENERAL CONSIDERATIONS

Some of the most basic facts in education can be easily overlooked because they are so evident. One such is fundamental to education, and common throughout OECD countries: in all of them, a major responsibility for the upbringing of young people is entrusted to a special institution – the school – with its specialised staff of professional teachers and other personnel. In all, attendance is compulsory by law. In all too, the minimum period that young people must remain before they can leave has been extended over the post-war period, sometimes significantly, so that it now covers a period of eight, nine or ten years. In some countries, such as Germany, the Netherlands, and Belgium, there is required attendance in at least part-time education up to the age of 18.

This represents an important slice of each person's lifetime. Thus, for a young person today who will live to be 75 years old, for example, at least one tenth of her or his life will have been spent in school. For the very many who go to pre-school and/or continue in post-compulsory education and training, this proportion is higher still. Indeed, with a total stay in education of 18-20 years no longer unusual, this represents approximately a quarter of the life of the 75 year-old. So, whereas education is often discussed as if it were essentially preparatory for subsequent roles and responsibilities – working life, active citizenship, the adult world – in fact, it is itself a major activity and period of the contemporary life span, and it now permeates the rest of the life cycle, not excluding retirement.

Two further basic facts, common across the OECD countries, closely follow from this. One is the sheer scale to which the educational enterprise has now grown. Very large sums of money are devoted to it. In many countries, public educational expenditure is 5, 6, or 7 per cent of GDP or greater, and 10-15 per cent or more of public expenditure. These figures are significantly higher again if account is taken of private expenditures, those on non-formal education and training, and expenditures on education and training made by other bodies and administrations. It is a major employer – of teaching staff, ancillary and back-up personnel, administrators. And, of course, the numbers of pupils and students enrolled in educational institutions at any one time are a very significant proportion of the total population. In the United States, for example, in fall 1981, nearly 58 millions were estimated to be enrolled in educational institutions with no less than 3 310 000 teachers[2].

These figures provide some perspective to the frequent charge that education systems are inefficient, bureaucratic and slow to change. However justified the claim often is, it would be surprising if such a large enterprise could readily adapt and shift from one year to the next;

and it is neglectful of its role as cultural anchor in rapidly changing societies to expect it to do so. They also provide perspective to the demands made on schools and educational administrations to be more accountable. It is clear that adequate accountability has to be established when so many public resources are devoted to, and so many occupied by, education today. The issues then are: accountable in what terms and to whom?

Another and closely related fact, whose importance is not diminished by its familiarity, is the extent of the expansion that education has undergone in recent times. No one indicator can adequately capture the scale of this change. One way that it can be illustrated is to compare levels of education between the older and younger members of the population. For example, over 7 out of 10 of those in their 50s and early 60s in Sweden in the mid-1970s had received less than 9 years' schooling. For the younger generation (aged 20-24 in 1979) the comparable figure was 5.5 per cent for men and 3.0 per cent for women[3]. Another way this can be illustrated is to chart the growth of university students over the short period of the mid-1960s to the beginning of the 1980s. University students in Germany almost tripled between 1965 and 1981. French university undergraduates rose from 331 000 to nearly 830 000 over the same period, and in Japan, the comparable 1981 figure of over 1 780 000 had risen from well under the one million mark in the mid-1960s. These are but single details of a general picture portraying a remarkable example of rapid social change which it is important to bear in mind in current discussions about the slowdown and even reversal of educational expansion.

These closely interrelated "facts" – the common experience of an extensive schooling, the sheer size of the educational enterprise, marked expansion over the last 2-3 decades – are shared across OECD countries. There are certain other fundamental facts these countries share, which are of a more qualitative nature but no less real. Throughout OECD countries, schooling for some young people is not a happy experience. They are obliged to remain in school, and some stay in post-compulsory provision, even though they patently do not enjoy it[4]. Under-achievement is not simply a relative concept. Achievement and motivation levels of many young people are low by any standard. The challenge posed by requiring longer school attendance for a certain group of youngsters who do not wish to remain, yet who have the right to a useful and personally relevant education, is explored throughout this report (in Chapter 6 in particular). The apparent anomaly of others who stay in education beyond the minimum school leaving age when they too do not enjoy it points to another basic reality common to all OECD countries: education systems throughout Member countries act as powerful devices of social sorting and selection[5]. Young people understand the general rule that the more successful they are in their acquisition of qualifications, the greater their chances of social advancement and economic security.

In spite of these common features, education systems of OECD countries are characterised by marked contrasts, divergences and differences. Illustrations of these differences serve as a useful reminder that identical patterns of development are the exception, not the rule. Most countries, for instance, have experienced the profound effects of the demographic "baby boom" bulge resulting from the birthrate peaks of the 1960s or early 1970s as it progressed from the lower to the higher levels of the education system and into the post-school world beyond, and are now endeavouring to cope with the subsequent rapid decline in births. But in Finland, the birthrate has steadily and consistently fallen over the last 30 years without peaks while in Ireland, apart from several small fluctuations, the pattern is the reverse. The birthrate has risen and continues to rise.

Another illustration of the variation between Member countries is provided by the proportion of young people finishing upper secondary school with the requisite qualifications to continue in higher education. The general trend over the 1970s and early 1980s is for this proportion to have risen. But this covers such widely disparate percentages as 87.0 in Japan and Norway (1981), 81.7 in Sweden (1982), 71.7 in the United States (1980), and 62.4 in Canada (1980) – the majority of the relevant age group – in contrast with 12.8 in Austria (1978), 19.3 in Portugal (1979), 10.5 in Turkey (1981), 26.3 in Germany (1982), 29.0 in Denmark (1983), 28.0 in France (1983), and 25.8 in the United Kingdom (1981) (see Table 1). These variations hide, of course, important differences in school structures and educational pathways, which in itself is another illustration of the educational diversity among Member countries. Equally marked differences arise in comparing the proportion of each country's GDP devoted to public educational expenditure. Education's percentage share of national wealth of 3.8 in Austria (1980), 4.5 in New Zealand (1981) and 5.0 in Japan (1981) compares with 7.1 in the Netherlands (1981), 7.7 in Belgium (1980), and 7.5 in Denmark (1978). Moreover, the directions of the trend are far from uniform. These proportions still rise in some countries, while falling significantly in others.

These general educational facts, portraying common fundamental features coexisting with contrasting developments, give context and qualification to the specific developments that are below, in this and in subsequent chapters.

THE DIFFERENT SECTORS OF EDUCATION: ENROLMENTS AND NUMBERS

In some countries, like Belgium, France, and the Netherlands, *pre-primary* education is the normal precursor of the compulsory primary school for most children. In some others, staying with the family, with perhaps other forms of childcare, remains the principal pre-school experience. But the dominant trend throughout the 1970s in all countries has been for rates of pre-primary enrolments to rise noticeably and, in some cases, dramatically. Thus, over the course of the decade, the rate of enrolment increased from 12.8 per cent to 50.3 per cent in Denmark and equally significantly in Sweden – from 30.5 to 83.4 per cent. In the other Scandinavian countries, Norway and Finland, the scale of the increase was only slightly less marked. A mere 6.6 per cent enrolment rate in 1970 had risen to 33.2 per cent in Norway by 1980, which was closely matched by the Finnish experience (9.4 to 30.7 per cent). The cases of Germany (39.6 to 82.6 per cent) and Greece (29.3 to 50.5) can also be singled out.

This growth of participation must be seen in relation to the diminishing total numbers of 3-, 4-, and 5-year-olds in many countries. In fact, the actual numbers of these very young pupils fell in certain cases (while enrolment rates rose) including countries mentioned above (Germany, Belgium, France and the Netherlands). Most recently, greater fluctuation can be observed in the number of births – in some cases increasing, in some stabilizing and in yet others, continuing to fall, though it should be noted that fertility rates have continued in an almost universal decline. These fluctuations make it extremely hazardous to predict how the size of the age group will change in Member countries in years to come.

Changes in pupil numbers in compulsory schooling, for obvious reasons, depend almost exclusively upon the ebbs and flows of demographic factors. Since births fell in many countries throughout the latter years of the 1960s, and in others since the beginning of the 1970s, numbers of pupils in *primary* education have been falling for several years already. The timing has varied and there are, as already seen, one or two exceptions, but the trend is general and is sometimes a marked one. The fall in enrolments provided the opportunity to reduce the average class size during the 1970s[6] and aggregate teacher/pupil ratios in primary schools

14

have improved almost everywhere. This is doubtless a positive development, both in terms of the quality of education, (irrespective of the inconclusive debate about the relation between classroom size and pupil achievement), and the protection of the teaching profession against unemployment.

It is worth recording the actual magnitude of the decline in primary pupil numbers that some countries have experienced as an illustration of the scale of problems faced, as well as opportunities presented by the decline of births and pupils. Between 1964 and 1978, the number of births practically halved in Germany (a 46 per cent drop), in the United Kingdom the fall was 34 per cent in the period 1964 to 1977, and 28 per cent in the United States between 1957 and 1973. And taking the most recent trends in births, several countries are expecting a severe drop in their primary pupil enrolments over the next several years: from 1982 to 1985/86, they can be expected to fall by 10 per cent or more in Australia, Denmark, France, Italy, the Netherlands, Norway and Sweden.

These demographic effects upon enrolments in *compulsory secondary* education are, of course, felt several years later. Already numbers in the age group are falling in several cases (Austria, Belgium, Canada, Finland, Germany, Greece, the Netherlands, Norway, Switzerland, the United Kingdom, the United States), so that by the end of this decade many Member countries will have to accommodate a severe decline in their student numbers in secondary schools. Indeed, the fall is expected to be as high as approximately a fifth to a quarter of 1982 levels by 1990 in Austria, Denmark, Germany, Italy, the Netherlands, Norway, Switzerland and the United Kingdom – a remarkable decline by any standard. The problems that changes of this scale pose for planning and the use of resources are acute. As with primary education, the latter years of the 1970s witnessed an improvement almost everywhere in pupil/teacher ratios. However, such a serious decline in student numbers is bound to have its effects on the size of the teaching force, hence posing the long-term problem of the ability of school systems to readjust should student numbers increase again towards the end of this century.

Demographic changes have figured prominently in the foregoing presentation, and one specific development within these aggregate trends deserves particular mention. School enrolments of *foreign children* and those of *migrants* have tended to increase even in countries where overall pupil numbers are falling, especially in pre-primary and primary education where these children are concentrated. Such is the divergence between the numbers of young nationals and foreigners coming into schools that its implications for the composition of schools will be far-reaching unless there is a sudden radical change in the fertility patterns of the different groups of the population.

With regard to *post-compulsory secondary* education, the general picture is one of continuing growth in participation rates and in the numbers in the corresponding age group. As usual, there are exceptions: in the United States, for example, participation has fallen slightly over recent years, but from a starting point of one of the countries with the highest proportion of young people staying on after the minimum leaving age. An important feature of the changing face of post-compulsory education and training is the growth of students in technical and vocational courses in a large number of Member countries. Here, too, there are important exceptions. In Germany, for example, with its vocational sector already highly developed, the picture is the reverse and it is the general branches that have predominantly grown. In certain other cases, general education still dominates provision, either because the vocational sector remains poorly developed or because professional preparation generally occurs afterwards in post-secondary or specialised institutions. But mostly, post-compulsory technical and vocational education grows. No less than with compulsory schooling, the demographic impact of falling numbers will be marked. Exactly what that impact will be, however, is more difficult to predict since this level of education and training is normally so diverse, since in many cases there remains wide scope for extending its coverage of the relevant age group, and because student participation is sensitive to the future, unpredictable labour market.

With the general growth of upper secondary education, the proportion of young people qualifying for entry to higher education has correspondingly grown. As Table 1 shows, the scale of change heralded by the 1970s was sometimes striking: within the space of ten years, the proportion of young people with the requisite qualifications has doubled in Finland and Germany and quadrupled in Spain. This is evidence of change that is both significant and swift.

Table 1. **Percentage of the age group with secondary school credentials qualifying for entry into higher education**
University and Non-university

Country	1970	Last year available	
Austria	15.3	(1978)	12.8
Canada	55.7	(1980)	62.4
Denmark	15.9	(1983)	29.0
Finland	20.6	(1981)	38.5
France	19.5[1]	(1983)	28.0[2]
Germany	11.3[3]	(1983)	26.3
Italy	33.5	(1981)	38.8
Japan	74.2	(1981)	87.0
Netherlands	35.4[4]	(1981)	43.5[5]
Norway[6]	23.1	(1981)	87.5
Portugal	16.3	(1979)	19.3
Spain	6.2	(1980)	24.1
Sweden	52.3[7]	(1982)	81.7[8]
Turkey	5.6	(1981)	10.5
United Kingdom (England and Wales)	21.4[9]	(1981)	25.8[10]
United States	75.7	(1980)	71.7
Yugoslavia	21.6	(1977)	32.8

1. Of which 16.2 per cent come from the Baccalauréat général and 3.3 per cent from Baccalauréat de technicien.
2. Of which 19.7 per cent come from the Baccalauréat général and 8.3 per cent from Baccalauréat de technicien.
3. Of which 10.8 per cent qualified for university education and 0.5 per cent for non-university education.
4. Of which 10.0 per cent qualified for university education and 25.4 per cent for non-university education.
5. Of which 11.6 per cent qualified for university education and 31.9 per cent for non-university education.
6. Artium Examination: Diploma of the 11th-12th year of schooling.
7. Of which 23.6 per cent came from 3/4-year lines of study and 28.7 per cent from 2-year lines of study.
8. Of which 31.6 per cent came from 3/4-year lines of study and 50.1 per cent from 2-year lines of study.
9. Of which 11.4 per cent qualified for university level studies and 10.0 per cent qualified for non-university level higher education.
10. Of which 13.1 per cent qualified for university level studies and 12.7 per cent for non-university education.
Source: *Education and Training, after Basic Schooling*, OECD, Paris, 1985, Chapter 5, Table 3.

The overall picture of expansion continues when attention turns to *higher education*. The broadening of access to the qualifications that grant admittance to it is mirrored by the growing numbers continuing their studies in universities and colleges. Table 2, showing the proportion of the age group at the end of their teens and early twenties who enter different forms of higher education, demonstrates that, with few exceptions, the 1970s and the early years of the 1980s remained a period of expanded coverage.

Three aspects of the developments revealed by Table 2 can be underlined. First, in contrast to the idea of higher education being an exclusive experience shared by the very select

Table 2. **Proportion of a generation[1] entering university-type (U) and non-university-type (NU) higher education**

Per 000

Country	1970	1975	1977	1979	1980	1981
Australia Universities	121(1973)	168	159	160	162	162
Colleges of Advanced Education U Level		68	94	111	117	127
Colleges of Advanced Education NU Level		128	96	85	81	79
Total		364	349	356	360	368
Austria U	88(1972)	86		122	126 P	132 P
NU				49	49	50
Total				171	175 P	182 P
Belgium U		118	130	135	129	129
Denmark U	118	175	147	143	145	
NU		178	156²	147²	182	
Total		353	303²	290²	327	
Finland U	116	160	151	157	187	
NU	77	95				
Total	193	255				
France U		218	213	217	213	225
NU³	38	57	74	102	105	115
Total		275	290	319	318	340
Germany U	116	144	135	133	139	148
NU	37	51	50	51	56	60
Total	153	195	185	184	195	208
Italy⁴ Total	256	311	292	271	276	251
Japan U	176	276	263	258	255	250
NU	67	114	113	112	110	108
Total	243	390	376	370	365	358
Netherlands⁴ U	83	85*	93	92	93	93
NU				166	165	164
Total				258	258	257
Spain U	145	198	206	166*	177	
NU		107	129	107*	106	
Total		305	335	273	283	
Sweden Total	229	248	228*	251		
United Kingdom Universities FT	83	91	94	93		
Universities FT and "Advanced Further Education"⁵	199		280	285		
United States U	309	279	274	279	278	279
NU	242	321	299	312	330	338
Total	551	600	573	591	608	617

P = Provisional
FT = Full-Time
* Indicates a change of classification.
1. Average of age groups normally corresponding to entry into higher education.
2. Without pre-primary teacher training.
3. As the number of institutions taken into account vary, data are not really comparable from year to year.
4. First year students.
5. Full-time and part-time for England and Wales only. Includes courses of university and non-university level.
Source: Educational Trends in the 1970s: A Quantitative Analysis, OECD, Paris, 1984.

few, it has in many places become a common educational path experienced by many. Although the United States with its system of mass higher education is untypical with over 6 out of every 10 young people entering college, it is now not unusual among Member countries for 2, 3 or more out of every 10 to enter higher education. Secondly, it is worth noting that the expansion of students continued despite the financial constraints felt by higher education increasingly towards the end of the 1970s. Considering actual numbers of students instead of proportions, the last decade saw substantial increases everywhere, sometimes very substantial indeed. Student enrolments more than doubled in Austria and Germany and even tripled in Spain. Most recently, however, there has been a slowing-down of growth in some countries both of the proportion of each generation continuing into higher education and of total student numbers. University student numbers have actually fallen in one or two cases. In Italy, for example, there were more than 7 per cent fewer new entrants in 1980 than in 1979. Thirdly, Table 2 shows well the marked differences in the degree to which higher education is a more common or more exclusive experience from one OECD country to another. Though these figures for new students can be misleading since they do not show how many drop out during their course (a substantial proportion in some countries), these variations remain significant.

A dominant feature in the development of higher education throughout the last 10-15 years has been the steady increase in the participation of women, who now figure on substantially more equal terms among the student population. Examining the female proportion of new university students, some examples of the increases evident since only the beginning of the 1970s give a measure of this change. Standing at 38.7 per cent in Australia in 1973, in only eight years the share of women had risen to 46.7 per cent. Similar percentage increases are 38.1 to 45.2 (Germany, 1970-1981), 37.8 to 46.2 (Austria, 1972-1979), 31.5 to 40.7 (Denmark, 1970-1980), 36.5 to 45.4 (Italy, 1970-1981), 21.6 to 35.4 (the Netherlands, 1970-1980), 31.9 to 39.5 (United Kingdom, 1970-1979). Spain is again a country where change has been particularly rapid. Here, women comprised only 28.1 per cent of new university students in 1970 but they were nearly half the new entrants by 1980 (46.4 per cent). These increases are important. But the figures do not show how women remain at a serious disadvantage throughout many parts of contemporary education systems. This is examined in greater detail in Chapter 4.

Table 2 does not show drop-outs nor, therefore, those who actually complete their courses. As the table is estimated on the basis of the age group of young people up to their early twenties, they also give only a partial picture of total enrolments, since higher education institutions admit ever larger numbers of older students (see Chapter 8). Reliable figures on the numbers of adult students are, unfortunately, rare, and are usually difficult to interpret. Nonetheless, the fact that there were over 21 million students in adult education in the United States in 1981, 1.2 million of whom were in full-time high school or college programmes[7] is a reminder that while solid facts may be sparse, education for adults represents a very substantial and growing portion of the total learning opportunities available in OECD countries.

AGGREGATE EDUCATIONAL EXPENDITURE PATTERNS

The evolution of public education expenditure is closely tied to demographic change. But it is also determined by many other factors, not least the political vicissitudes which determine overall public spending at any given time, and particularly the distribution of public expenditure among the various social sectors. The more detailed patterns and trends of educational expenditure are elaborated in Chapter 9. Here, three of the aggregate trends are presented.

First, as countries have become more affluent, so have substantially larger sums been devoted to education. Even if educational expenditure had remained constant as a *proportion of GDP*, the increase would have been large. In fact, educational expenditure grew as a share of GDP in real terms in many countries during the 1960s and at least up to the mid-1970s. As noted above, there are wide variations between countries as to the actual size of education's share and there are also exceptions to the trend. Nevertheless, up to about 1975 education received a growing slice of a growing cake. Thereafter, this share has tended to decline – in some countries more sharply than others. Though data for the most recent years are not generally available, this downward trend seems to persist in a large number of OECD countries.

Secondly, as a *share of public expenditure,* educational spending in real terms also grew in the 1960s and into the 1970s reflecting the rapid growth of education systems and the priority that education received. Similarly, this share tends now to be declining, albeit slightly in some cases, and again with exceptions. Thirdly, as a *proportion of social expenditure* (which also includes pensions, health care, family and other allowances and unemployment insurance) the position of educational spending has significantly changed in the last two decades. Taking the seven major OECD countries as the basis (the United States, Japan, Germany, Canada, France, Italy, and the United Kingdom), in 1960 education made up nearly 30 per cent of social expenditure. This was almost equal to the portion devoted to pensions[8]. It is now only a little over a fifth of social expenditure, less than the spending on health care and far less than the 37 per cent now given to pensions[8]. It is clear, however, that a large part of this shift reflects the increasing costs of these other major items of public expenditure. In all of these seven countries, too, social expenditure represented a much larger proportion of GDP in 1981 than it did twenty years before – this proportion more than doubled in the United States and Japan.

NEW SOCIO-ECONOMIC REALITIES

This section focuses on some of the main economic developments that form an important backcloth to education and are generally more quantifiable and amenable to statistical summary compared with the more conventionally "social". This is not to suggest that social changes are less important, and they are discussed extensively in the following chapters. Nor should it be forgotten that such "economic" phenomena as economic growth, unemployment, working hours, and the labour market participation of different groups, including young people and women, have far-reaching social causes and consequences.

One evident and fundamental fact is that OECD countries are societies that generally are affluent. They have grown still more affluent over the 1970s and into the 1980s despite the recurrent economic recession, though there are marked inequalities in the distribution of wealth and income in each. Between 1970 and 1973 and between 1975 and 1979, real GDP yearly growth for OECD countries as a whole was 5.1 and 4.1 per cent respectively, and while such growth has been much smaller or negligible in certain other years and in a number of countries, the general picture is one of increasing economic affluence[9]. Alongside this, a further feature of "post-industrial" societies is that people are employed increasingly in services, rather than the primary and secondary sectors of agriculture and industry. Since the mid-1970s and up to 1981, employment in services grew by 20 million throughout OECD countries while falling by 3 million in agriculture. Employment in the industrial sector did expand by 3.6 million in the latter years of the 1970s, but fell by well over a million in 1980-81. As usual, such aggregates mask important variations between countries, but the general picture is a clear one.

The other side of this picture is the persistence of unacceptably high levels of unemployment, perhaps the biggest single economic problem now facing OECD countries. It has grown alarmingly over the 1970s and 1980s, particularly over recent years, as graphically portrayed by the *OECD Employment Outlook:*

"The unemployment situation in the OECD area has deteriorated dramatically since the beginning of 1980 ... In 1981, there were 24 and 3/4 million people unemployed in the OECD area (an unemployment rate of 6.7 per cent), more than double the 1973 level. The latest estimates suggest that this increased to 30 million in 1982, or an unemployment rate of 8.1 per cent."[10]

While unemployment generally has profound implications for education, of particular significance are the special difficulties facing young people in the labour market today. Compared with the general unemployment rate of 8.1 per cent, unemployment was more than double at 16.5 per cent for young people up to the age of 24 years in 1982, representing some 9 million out-of-work youngsters in the seven major OECD countries. In certain cases, the youth unemployment rate was considerably higher still. In Italy, for example, it stood at 29.8 per cent in 1982 and was higher again in Spain at 36.9 per cent – that is, nearly 4 out of every 10 young people in this case were without work. A new feature of the recent worsening of the labour market prospects of young people is that, whereas before teenagers were particularly badly hit relative to adults in their early twenties, the situation of 20-24 year-olds has now grown significantly worse[11]. Moreover, long-term unemployment has become more common among young people, a departure from the traditional pattern of relatively short spells out of work. In Belgium, France, and the Netherlands, half or more of the young unemployed have been without work for 6 months or longer. In sum, the unemployment situation of young people well into their twenties is a bleak one indeed.

The effects and consequences of this for education are many, as discussed in the next chapter. One fact needs underlining here: the risk of unemployment is much higher for those with few or no educational qualifications. The correlation is by no means perfect and the employment position of higher education graduates has also worsened in recent years. Nevertheless, the relation is clear, as the following examples show. Among out-of-work Australian teenagers in 1981, no less than 63 per cent of them had incomplete secondary education. Unemployment rates of 10.3 per cent and 12.5 per cent in 1982 among university and other higher education graduates respectively up to the age of 24 in Canada, contrasts with 20 per cent for those with no higher education, and nearly 32 per cent for young people with just the minimum years of schooling. In France in 1982, among the long-term unemployed under the age of 30, less than 3 per cent were graduates of higher education and only 5 and a half per cent had completed long-cycle upper secondary schooling. Long-term unemployment, in other words, is concentrated among young people who have had a minimum education or who had left shortly after the minimum school-leaving age[12].

Compared with unemployment, the reduction of working time has quite different implications for education. The growth of non-working time is a complex subject , and the pitfalls of interpretation are many, but its reality cannot be gainsaid. The *OECD Employment Outlook* summarises it thus:

"The data show that annual hours worked have decreased substantially in all these countries [twelve Member countries] over the past two decades and this decline is continuing almost everywhere. Since the mid-1970s, however, there has been a general slowdown in the trend rate of decline. Contrary to what might have been expected, in many cases this slowdown has continued during the present recession ... Reductions in the normal work week and increases in annual paid holidays were major factors in the secular decline in annual working hours. Structural changes in the composition of employment and labour supply which have combined in favour of part-time working were also important."[13]

Part-time workers are predominantly female in most countries, and this raises another major development – the growth in the numbers of women in the labour force. This increase has been one of the most notable socio-economic changes of the last 2-3 decades, the magnitude of which can be seen from the global figures that introduce a recent OECD report on the subject:

"[There has been a] dramatic global development of female participation in the labour market over the last 30 years. While the number of economically active men in OECD countries increased by 25 per cent over this period, the comparable figure for women was 74 per cent.... The actual figures are these. The total labour force of OECD countries increased by 28 million in the 1950s, by 30 million in the 1960s and by 43 million in the 1970s. In the first two decades, women's contribution to the increase was slightly more than half – 51.7 and 51.2 per cent – whereas in the last decade it amounted to 63.2 per cent. By 1980, there were 136 million economically active women in the OECD countries out of a total active population of 351 million."[14]

The significantly increased participation rates of women in the labour force have widespread implications for education and training that relate directly both to the economic and social position of women today and to their children. The special problems that still confront women in the labour market – low pay, the high degree of segmentation into male and female occupations with very limited opportunities for women to get managerial promotion, and the particular vulnerability of women to job changes consequent on economic restructuring – also have important educational implications. Educational issues raised range from the availability of pre-school provision through to training and retraining for non-traditional occupations and high-level jobs. It should be noted that the greatly increased participation of women in the labour market provides serious qualification to the general trend of reduced working hours described above. Far from implying greater leisure time, the fact that there are more women in paid work means that for many it means doing two "jobs" – one at work during the day, and another, no less onerous, of running a home as well, leaving less free time than enjoyed either by men or by women who are not in the labour market.

The facts, statistics and developments presented in this chapter have necessarily been both highly selective and illustrative. They do, however, encapsulate the more salient features of the overall condition of education today in its social and economic setting, and thus provide a background against which the following chapters can elaborate more specific analysis of future educational policy issues.

NOTES AND REFERENCES

1. This chapter is based largely on the statistics contained in the two reports *Educational Trends in the 1970s: A Quantitative Analysis*, OECD, Paris, 1984 and *Resource Redeployment in Education*, OECD, Paris (forthcoming).

2. *Digest of Education Statistics*, National Center for Education Statistics, Washington D.C., 1982, Tables 1 and 7.

3. *Levnadsförhallanden Arsbok 1975*, Table 75; and *Perspektiv pa valfarden 1982*, Table 6.14.

4. See *Education and Work: The Views of the Young*, OECD/CERI, Paris, 1983.

5. *Selection and Certification in Education and Employment*, OECD, Paris, 1977.

6. *Compulsory Schooling in a Changing World*, OECD, Paris, 1983, Table 3.

7. *Digest of Education Statistics, 1982, op. cit.,* Table 141.

8. "Social Expenditure: Erosion or Evolution?", in *The OECD Observer* No. 126, January 1984.

9. Most of the evidence in this section comes from the *OECD Employment Outlook*, OECD, Paris, September 1983.

10. *OECD Employment Outlook, op. cit.,* pp. 21 and 23.

11. *New Policies for the Young*, OECD, Paris (forthcoming).

12. *Chômeurs de longue durée*, Agence nationale pour l'Emploi, Paris, 1982.

13. *OECD Employment Outlook, op. cit.,* pp. 41-42.

14. *The Employment and Unemployment of Women in OECD Countries*, OECD, Paris, 1984, p. 10.

Part Two

THE SOCIO-ECONOMIC ENVIRONMENT OF EDUCATION

Chapter 3

EDUCATION, THE LABOUR MARKET, AND STRUCTURAL CHANGE

THE POTENTIAL AND LIMITS OF THE EDUCATIONAL RESPONSE

Faced by the magnitude of the economic problems and change, whose main features were only partially sketched in the previous chapter, education's role is potentially far-reaching. It is widely recognised that education (including training) supports the economy and can shape its performance and development. Modern economies require, more than ever before, high levels of skill and flexibility of the labour force. Longer-term structural and technological evolution imply a growing and central capacity in society for learning and relearning. Human resources are crucial. Conversely, the economic and employment situation influences not only the resources made available for education, but ideas and expectations about the usefulness of education and demands for various types of educational provision. In particular, the problem of massive unemployment, and the realities of labour market segmentation that affect certain groups so harshly, call for a substantial education and training response.

But though critical, education and training are not panaceas. The OECD Intergovernmental Conference on *Employment Growth in the Context of Structural Change,* held in February 1984, recognised that the prime source of improvement in labour market conditions must be general macro-economic recovery and growth[1]. Education, training and labour market policies are only complementary to this, though very necessary complements. On the specific major problem of youth unemployment, the OECD Education Committee has also drawn the limits of education's task:

"The main contribution to creating and improving jobs has to come from the economic and employment policies of governments and from the investment, production and personnel policies of enterprises. The main role of education and training in relation to the labour market is the important supporting one of preparing young people for their lives at work. To some extent, it can also help reduce unemployment but this is not its main task."[2]

In a context of change in the structure of jobs and work processes, and in the composition and demands of the labour force, this task is, of course, the broader one that includes education, training and retraining for people of all ages, not only the young. As will be seen throughout this chapter, the economic arguments supporting a strategy of recurrent education are even more forceful and applicable now than they were in the optimistic days of the early 1970s when recurrent education was a byword for educational reform[3].

However, alongside the general understanding of the importance of learning and relearning to healthy economic performance is the fact that the neat, often simplistic, economic theories of education have not well survived since the 1960s. Certain reasons for this are examined below. In brief, it can be said that the complexity of the labour market, the unpredictability of its future development, and the multi-faceted, often diffuse, way that education functions in it do not permit the precise prescriptions that once were made about the planning of education's contribution to the economy.

In examining education in relation to the labour market and to structural and technological change, two perspectives can be distinguished. The first focuses on an examination of the functioning of educational certificates in the labour market and the varying fortunes of those with different levels of education. This perspective is thus concerned not so much with education's role in promoting economic goals such as productivity or flexibility, but rather with its importance as a powerful agent of selection in the distribution of economic rewards. Secondly, in addressing the centrality of human resources to structural and technological change, education's productive, rather than distributive, potential comes to the fore. Though the precise contribution of education in these two perspectives is often far from clear, distinguishing the two helps to clarify the potential of, as well as the limits to, an educational response to the economic challenges and perplexing difficulties that are confronted today.

UNDERSTANDING THE LINKS BETWEEN EDUCATION AND THE ECONOMY: CHANGING PERSPECTIVES OVER THE LAST TWO DECADES

The 1961 Washington Conference on Economic Growth and Investment in Education[4] was one sign of the gathering belief that educational expansion was a powerful motor of economic growth, that foreseen rates of growth would enable OECD countries to respond to rising levels of social demand for education, and that such an expansion of education would contribute to equality of opportunity. The idea that educational achievement leads to personal advancement and financial reward was embodied in the various forms of human capital theory that flourished at the time[5]. They started from the assumption that education is a major investment comparable with that in physical capital for the benefit of both society and individuals. With a sizeable proportion of economic growth unaccounted for by technical advance and physical investment, the "residual" of human investment (predominantly through education) seemed the main reason for increasing affluence[6]. In countries at the earlier stages of economic development, manpower forecasting went further in attempting not only to estimate the general economic benefits of education to society but to show where educational investment should be made. Based on predictions of future manpower needs, educational investments could then be made to avoid mismatches of supply and demand and hence maximise economic performance[7]. There were many different approaches – often based on sophisticated theories – and they were never presented as a single, coherent whole. Together, however, they provided powerful economic argument for educational expansion.

Subsequent developments, in the economy and society as well as the disciplines that study them, have tended to underline just how complex is the education-economy relationship, making many of the assumptions of these approaches, sophisticated as they are, appear simplistic. One fact is that growth faltered with the recessions of 1973, 1979 and the early

26

1980s, at the very time when, according to the theories, countries should have been reaping the economic benefits of rapid educational expansion. Though few contended that education alone guarantees growth, the confidence of earlier economic theories of education was undermined. Approaches such as manpower forecasting, that are based on making prognoses of educational needs from predictions of the changes in the occupational structure, have largely fallen from fashion since the 1960s. They tend to beg too many questions about the relationship between the structure of occupations and the educational requirements of jobs as well as suffering from very large problems, conceptual and technical, of making forecasts of the future[8]. Another factor is the more widespread questioning of the competitive market assumptions that underpinned so many of the economic theories of education. More social and institutional explanations of labour markets developed; notably, theories of the job queue[9], labour market segmentation and the "dual" labour market[10]. The growing acceptance of more institutional labour market theories of the "job queue", and education's role in powerfully influencing each person's position in the "queue", is shown by the account given in the *OECD Employment Outlook* of long-term unemployment:

"In slack labour markets, even well qualified and adaptable persons may enter the ranks of the long-term unemployed either because there are virtually no jobs available or because of competition from other unemployed workers for what jobs exist. During any given period there will be a flow of people into unemployment. People with the most competitive skills and potential productivity will be selected out during the course of the first few months. Those who are left will then face competition from more recent arrivals into the unemployment pool, many of whom will have characteristics which will allow them to move to the top of the hiring queue, ahead of those who have been unemployed for longer. The effect is that the least competitive among the unemployed are pushed farther and farther down the hiring queue and into long-term unemployment."[11]

As seen in Chapter 2, the lack of educational credentials increases greatly the chances of being, and staying, unemployed.

How far more institutional approaches are actually theories is an open question. Equally, "screening hypotheses" – based on the idea that employers, particularly when there are plentiful candidates for scarce jobs, use educational certificates to screen as a principal form of selection – do not amount to an alternative "theory" of labour markets. What they have done, however, is seriously to question the basic assumptions of competitive labour markets that underpinned the earlier approaches, by drawing attention to the importance of the social and institutional realities of employer hiring practices, pathways and barriers in the job market and the inequalities of opportunity that these give rise to. None of these approaches questions the fact that the person with higher levels of educational qualification, on average, earns more and is at a competitive advantage over the less qualified.

Closely related to these are the analyses that attacked the very heart of the "first-generation" economics of education – the assumption that education, through the provision of cognitive, technical knowledge and skills, directly enhances economic productivity. The attack came from at least two directions. There were those who claimed, in line with the notion of "screening", that employers use credentials as a blanket form of selection, leaving untested and unknown the degree to which the better educationally qualified are in fact more qualified for the job in question[12]. Some went further to claim that those with higher levels of education were often actually less productive[13]. These analyses can be distinguished from those that questioned the idea that it is through the possession of cognitive, technical knowledge and skills that employers' preference for the educated persons comes. One reason for this stems from the common-sense observation that much of the content of the school syllabus is neither of direct applicability in the work adults engage in, nor is it remembered.

Furthermore, increasing interest has come to be given to the role of education in imparting non-cognitive traits, on which some place equal or greater importance than technical knowledge. These are the traits of habits, behaviour, and attitudes that employers value and which education engenders through its "hidden curriculum". Some radical critics have taken this a step further by arguing that employers value the more educated worker not because of his greater knowledge but because the "legitimate" hierarchy of educational credentials reinforces the unequal authority structure of modern enterprises.

How do these many strands of argument leave today's understanding of the relationship between education and the economy? Do they undermine the potential of education to provide a significant response to contemporary economic problems and challenges? On the contrary, education and training are more than ever central to modern economies that are based upon rapidly changing knowledge and skills, many of them highly complex. But they have drawn attention to the sheer complexity of education's economic role that derives, among other factors, from the social and institutional nature of labour markets and certification and from the "hidden curriculum" of education that develops the attitudes and non-cognitive skills of importance at work, possibly as much as knowledge and skills for sound economic performance. Various aspects of education's economic role are considered in the following sections, including the implications for education of changes in employment structures, unemployment, working time and technological development.

CHANGES IN EMPLOYMENT STRUCTURES

While unemployment is the outstanding economic problem of today, it must be remembered that *employment* has risen significantly throughout the last decade. The number of jobs in the OECD area as a whole grew by over 33 million between 1970 and 1982, reflecting in part the demographic influx into the labour force, the greatly increased numbers of working women, and the impact of migration and immigration. But the structure of employment has changed, in line with developments in the patterns of production, by industry, regions, and occupations. The very rapid growth of the service sector was described in Chapter 2. Public sector growth was particularly important for the influx of the more highly educated coming into the job market. The proportion who are self-employed has declined as have the semi- and unskilled and agricultural workers. The growth in overall employment, however, should be considered in order to put these relative changes into perspective. For example, there were a million more labourers in the United States in 1980 than in 1960, even though their share of the labour force fell from 5 to 4.4 per cent[14].

One of the most significant structural shifts in OECD countries witnessed over the last two decades has been the expansion of part-time employment:

"Part-time work has grown in importance in all OECD countries over the last two decades. This is especially so since the first oil shock: in many countries, particularly in Europe, part-time employment has continued to grow when full-time employment has been stagnating or even declining. Indeed, on a net jobs basis, in Europe one out of every two new jobs created since the first oil shock was a part-time job compared to only about one out of every five new jobs in North America... the continued shift in the structure of OECD economies towards the service sector is a major determinant of part-time employment. The nature of many service sector activities is particularly suited to the use of part-time labour in the production process. Part-time employment, especially among females, is heavily concentrated in the service sector."[15]

Even this brief summary of the main structural changes of employment that have occurred over the last twenty years or so provides serious qualification to the heralded arrival of "post-industrial" societies where it was thought that jobs would increasingly be highly skilled and education would be paramount, as communication and the manipulation of words and numbers come to replace the manufacture of physical products in the modern economy. This is happening to some degree as discussed below. But there still remain large numbers of low-skilled jobs. Labour markets have seen an influx of young people and migrants, for example, many of whom have had to accept unstable and poorly-paid work, often marginal to the labour market. And part-time employment dominated by female workers has grown – part-time employment that is typically poorly paid, without fringe benefits comparable with full-time workers and, in some countries, is not covered by employment protection legislation. Although it may be an oversimplification to describe the labour market as "dual", divided into a primary, well-protected sector and a secondary sector, typified by low pay and poor security, it is clear that there are major segments and barriers that are extremely difficult to cross. The fruits of the "post-industrial" society are not shared by everyone.

Simply extending educational opportunities cannot erase these barriers, though it can contribute to a more even distribution of the different social groups between these sectors – young compared with prime-age workers, women compared with men, migrants and immigrants compared with nationals. This alone is not an insignificant task for education and training. It becomes all the more important since there are signs that the developments towards a "dual" economy appear to be growing:

> "There is some evidence of a deliberate shift in enterprise manpower policy towards greater use of temporary labour, much of which is part-time. This permits employers to match labour input to actual and expected output fluctuations while, at the same time, maintaining a relatively stable core of trained workers who have a high degree of job security."[16]

This underlines the responsibility of public education authorities in the provision of training and retraining, particularly for the sections of the population who are most likely to be employed outside the primary sector of the labour market. Their jobs typically do not have a training component nor form part of an established career path, where training is naturally a part. Being more marginal and temporary, structural changes and economic fluctuations for them result in job losses rather than retraining for new tasks. At present, training for many occupations can be obtained only by securing the job that brings the training with it, and these jobs are in great demand. The training organised by public authorities has the advantage that it can be in more general areas than the specific training that enterprises will tend to provide. There is the additional argument, relevant to the discussion of unemployment below, that it is the public authorities who are in a position to develop training as an anti-cyclical device, giving workers who risk losing their jobs or without work the preparation in new knowledge and skills during times of unemployment in order that they are better prepared and better placed in the job queue when recovery begins.

THE EDUCATIONAL RESPONSE TO UNEMPLOYMENT

The alarming scale of current unemployment has been described in Chapter 2 as have the particular hardships faced today by young people coming out of education. Women are increasingly vulnerable to unemployment. Their levels of employment grew through the 1960s

29

and 1970s and was less sensitive to cyclical changes. But now, with high levels of general unemployment and with large numbers of working women, often highly concentrated in "female" occupations[17] and in sectors that are vulnerable to structural change, their unemployment rates are higher throughout OECD countries (exceptions being Finland, Japan, Ireland, and the United Kingdom).[18]

Long-term unemployment has become a disturbing feature of the current economic situation and a wide range of less advantaged groups have been severely affected:

"Long-term unemployment has increased rapidly in most OECD countries in recent years, rising broadly as unemployment has risen but more rapidly in recessions. In several European countries, those unemployed for over a year are 30 per cent or more of total unemployed. The proportion is much lower in North America, and in low-unemployment countries. A high proportion of the unemployed are young people and, reflecting this, a substantial proportion of the long-term unemployed are young people, although the proportion varies markedly from country to country. However, the incidence of unemployment is greatest for older people. In general, the groups most affected are the old, the sick, and those with below-average or out-dated skills. Nevertheless, as the overall incidence of long-term unemployment increases, it begins to affect other groups more severely, including skilled and professional workers."[19]

Thus, the picture of a "dual" labour force, with a relatively well-protected and remunerated primary sector and a much more vulnerable secondary sector, becomes even more striking when account is taken of the extent and distribution of unemployment. It cannot be sufficiently emphasized that it is not the responsibility of education and training to resolve such widespread economic and social problems. But in making a full contribution to help the many who risk being left aside in the labour market, a substantial programme of preparation for work as part of a widely developed set of opportunities for continuing or recurrent education is essential.

One important component of this, that inevitably falls largely under the responsibility of public authorities, are programmes in the basic skills of literacy and numeracy. Although any estimate of the extent of illiteracy is beset by problems of definition and measurement, it has been calculated that some 8 million people over the age of 15 in France are incapable of reading a short and simple text related to their daily life[20]. Since there is no reason to suppose that France has an illiteracy problem of greater magnitude than other countries, this gives some measure of education's most basic task. Many adults are deficient even in the skills of reading, let alone more sophisticated vocational skills.

Education that is directly relevant to work must, however, be the main component of the response. The educational responses to unemployment are many but one critical area has been identified to be middle-level skills, and as Chapter 7 explains, this has been a gap in the provision of many countries. More basically, the aim should be to allow all who have failed to acquire secondary level qualifications the chance to do so. Clearly, to attract back those who deliberately left the education system without successfully completing a certified course will require innovative, attractive courses as well as clear, readily available information about their existence and content.

Particularly with the growing recognition of the pitfalls inherent in manpower forecasting, Member countries have sought to develop alternative, more practice-based approaches to the planning of education and training in relation to the labour market. They include attempts to identify skills that are common to a range of jobs or occupations; to group training into fewer and more generic categories; and to identify what makes skills transferable. All of these call for empirical analyses which are not yet conclusive. But investigations have at least underlined the importance of ensuring high-quality technical training based on self-directed learning and personal development, and of endowing people with a sufficient knowledge of the labour market to be able to recognise opportunities to change their jobs or seek new ones, develop their skills and improve their incomes. To this end, there is a need for more extensive preparation for working life during compulsory education, and for improved counselling for students of all ages.

Similarly, greater opportunities for adult training and retraining is a priority. The training capacity of the public institutions has been built up in relation to the lower levels of unemployment of the post-war years when there was less need for policies to promote the structural redeployment of the labour force. Policies in this area should help retrain older workers, often immobilised geographically by the costs of moving and by social and family ties, through further skill training which preserves the value of their accumulated experience and helps them compete with other workers on a broadly equal basis.

Assessing the kinds of education and training that will best respond to economic goals is very complex. Since partial explanation of the role education plays in personal social advancement is simply the advantage of possessing educational credentials that employers use to screen for jobs, the contradiction that this implies, were education expected to "resolve" unemployment, is clear. If everyone possesses the requisite credentials, they no longer act as an effective filter and other, "higher" credentials are then demanded or else other sorts of criteria come into play. Assessing the best educational response is rendered still more difficult because the reason why employers will tend to be attracted towards the better-qualified job applicant extends well beyond the fact that he or she is believed to possess more of the knowledge acquired from the school curriculum.

It is thus important to distinguish the credential and the instrinsic value of education and its cognitive from its non-cognitive and more general functions. While technical knowledge and skills are undoubtedly important for many jobs, this is not only, or even mainly, in the specific form they were originally learned. More generic skills and general capacities, such as the ability to adapt knowledge to different situations and "learning to learn" are required. General education is crucial, therefore, but to be truly "general" today, this cannot exclude work preparation in favour of the purely academic. Emphasis needs to be given to the development of programmes that reach a new balance between what are traditionally regarded as general and vocational. As emphasized in Chapters 6 and 7, preparation in overly specific and narrow professional skills will often prove of little benefit, particularly in a world of rapid structural change where they become quickly out-dated.

It is increasingly recognised that the widely-held traditional distinction between general education, thought to develop mainly cognitive and affective aptitudes, and vocational education (or training) that mainly confers specific skills, is a false one. The OECD Intergovernmental Conference on Vocational Education and Training in 1978 concluded that a convergence should be, and is, taking place between the two[21]. The problem remains that, in most countries, the status attached to general and to vocational education is different and is deeply-rooted in social attitudes.

Concerning the importance of the "hidden curriculum" in developing non-cognitive and personality traits, and affective capacities such as work habits and modes of behaviour, it is more difficult to see how educational policy can respond directly. Can schools explictly teach punctuality or neatness and, indeed, should they? If particular stress were laid upon these characteristics in a school's régime, they could easily conflict with other desirable aims, such as self-discovery, learning to learn, and student motivation, as well as other educational objectives. Some of the most useful things that a school gives its students in preparing them for the world of work may therefore lie in its intangible "ethos" that is particularly hard to define and still more difficult to replicate generally through educational policies.

BROAD CHANGES IN WORKING TIME

Table 3 broadly shows recent trends in annual hours worked in a number of OECD countries. The general picture is that work time is falling – in some countries significantly, in others less so. Historically, the 1950s and well into the 1960s were years of stability and sometimes even of increase in work time, associated particularly with the post-war reconstruction. It was only the late 1960s and 1970s that saw a quickening general movement towards its reduction. In several countries, weekly hours have altered less than annual hours and some groups typically work longer than others. It should also be noted that time away from work is not necessarily "free" and this is particularly well illustrated by the case of working mothers who usually combine onerous domestic duties in the evenings and weekends with their job in the paid labour market. Nevertheless, the trend is a clear one: time spent at work is falling. While it is true that many activities compete for people's time, and some will choose simply to have more relaxation, a large and exciting new potential for education, particularly education for adults, is being opened.

Table 3. **Average actual hours worked per person in employment**[1]

Average annual growth rates in percentages

Country	1973-75	1975-79	1979-82	1980	1981	1982
Canada	−0.8	−0.6	−1.0	−0.6	−0.9	−1.5
Finland	−0.8	−0.3	−1.0	−1.3	−0.6	−1.1
France	−1.4	−0.5	−2.0	0.3	−1.4	−4.8
Germany	−1.9	−0.5	−0.6	−0.7	−1.0	0.0
Japan	−3.0	0.6	−0.3	−0.3	−0.4	−0.2
Italy	−1.6	0.1	−0.3	−0.6	0.1	−0.7
Netherlands	−2.8	−1.4	0.6	0.2	0.5	0.7
Norway	−0.6	−1.7	−0.4	−0.1	−1.2	0.0
Sweden	−1.3	−0.2	−0.8	0.8	0.6	0.9
United Kingdom	1.1	−0.9	−1.6	−2.5	−3.2	0.9
United States	−1.2	−0.1	−0.8	−0.8	−0.3	−1.1
Seven major countries	−1.8	−0.1	−0.7	−0.7	−0.6	−0.8
Four major European countries	−1.7	−0.4	−1.1	−0.8	−1.3	−1.1

1. These data refer, as far as possible, to the total economy, with the exception of Japan where data refer to employees in enterprises with 30 or more employees; the Netherlands, where data refer to persons employed in the private enterprise sector excluding agriculture and fishing; and the United States, where data for 1973-81 include employees only, whereas for 1981-82 data refer to gross weekly hours of production or non-supervisory workers on private non-agricultural payrolls.
Source: *Employment Outlook*, OECD, Paris, 1984, Table 10.

Work-time changes for the whole lifespan have perhaps more far-reaching long-term consequences for education. While in absolute terms, because of greater longevity over the last several decades, the total number of years that comprise working careers may be longer than they were, in relative terms, the ratio of working life to the total lifespan has shifted in the opposite direction. This is due largely to three main factors: the increased longevity of the population (though the increase has been less marked in recent years), the more extensive periods spent in education before entering the labour market as witnessed by the post-war expansion of education systems, and the tendency for retirement and partial or total withdrawal from the labour market to come earlier in life than before.

As work becomes increasingly compressed into the middle period of people's lives, one of its results has been that the elderly have become a much larger section of the population than before. As societies come to confront this challenge, it should be realised how important education is as a major activity for older people. Going further, the diminishing proportion represented by work over the life-cycle raises the prospect of other activities and occupations becoming personally and socially elevated to a level comparable to that now enjoyed exclusively by work. Definitions of self, and of socially useful activity, which have been dominated by this one criterion, can come increasingly to find a place for others. And education is foremost for such personal and social elevation, though, without significant change in the present organisation of educational resources and opportunities to enable adults to enjoy education on a recurrent basis, this potential will be significantly impaired.

THE LABOUR MARKET AND INCOME REWARDS
OF HIGHER EDUCATION GRADUATES

Having focused throughout much of the preceding sections upon those who are disadvantaged in the current economic situation and labour market, it is worthwhile to look briefly at the situation of those at the other end of the scale: higher education graduates. The fact that more education brings with it, on average, personal economic benefit in the form of higher incomes, better jobs, more secure employment status and fringe benefits, is well known. This association between education and earnings can be expressed in different ways – average earnings differentials by educational level, rates-of-return to education, correlation coefficients – all of which convey essentially the same information. In the 1960s, the earnings advantage of the higher education graduate was clear, as Table 4 shows, but more recent analyses suggest that some of this income advantage has been eroded. The main change appears to have occurred in the early part of the 1970s, stabilizing in the latter half of the decade. It has been suggested, however, in relation to evidence from the United States, that it can be misleading to view changes only since the end of the 1960s as evidence of the long-term erosion of the relative economic advantage of higher education graduates[14]. Instead, the end of the 1960s and early 1970s can be seen as a high point so that their position now is similar to that before the massive expansion of higher education in the 1960s.

Table 4. **Index of average annual earning of labour by level of education in the 1960s**

Country	Year	Educational Level		
		Primary	Secondary	Higher
Belgium	1960	100	251	502
Canada	1961	100	144	263
France	1968	100	183	289
Greece	1960	100	139	220
Italy	1969	100	141	244
Japan	1968	100	117	161
Netherlands	1965	100	131	152
Norway	1966	100	140	213
United States	1967	100	129	200
United Kingdom	1967	100	140	225

Source: G. Psacharopoulos, *Earnings and Education in OECD Countries,* OECD, Paris, 1975, Table 7.1

Certain reasons for the decline of the relative earnings advantage of graduates are not difficult to find: the rapid growth of their supply, coupled with high levels of unemployment, have meant that more have been forced to take lower-paid jobs than they did previously; they are young compared with the general population and their earnings consequently lower, and there are many more female graduates now than in the 1960s and their average earnings are still well below those of men in all OECD countries. Demand, as well as supply, factors have probably contributed. Can it thus be concluded that it no longer "pays" to acquire an extensive education? The answer is definitely in the negative. The very vulnerable labour market position of those with low levels of qualification is emphasized throughout this report. However, it is true that the labour market opportunities for higher education graduates are changing and, for some, worsening[22].

An important contributing factor to their worsened position on the demand side (demand for labour) has been the restrictions of growth in public services and other sources of employment dependent upon public funds. Certain of these sectors, (like teaching that has been such a significant employer of graduates), have been severely cut back. This has particularly affected female graduates, many of whom have relied upon teaching for jobs after they leave college. Furthermore, the differences in labour market prospects of graduates from the various branches and institutions of higher education have become greater. An academic education, and one in the arts, humanities, and pure sciences particularly, is generally favoured less by employers for high-level jobs, especially in the private sector to which many more graduates are now having to turn for employment. The declining earnings value of higher education may, however, be partly apparent rather than real. To the extent that employers' preferences have changed towards more professionally-oriented courses rather than the traditional full-length university degree, then so have student choices (see Chapter 8). Comparison of the earnings of higher education graduates as a whole over the last twenty years may thus be misleading: a high level of qualification may still command comparable financial rewards but the relevant type of qualification has changed.

EDUCATION AND TECHNOLOGICAL CHANGE

Few subjects arouse such a bewildering variety of predictions as the employment and skill implications of technological change. Some pessimistically predict that its labour-saving effects will mean that "human workers will go the way of the horse". Others stress the increases in productivity consequent upon the introduction and widespread use of new technologies as well as the improvement of the quality of products and services that could lead to a growth of demand and new investment. New, but different, kinds of jobs will be created, so it is argued. Others again are more cautious, arguing that employment growth is possible but on condition that certain significant changes are realised. At the recent OECD international conference on *Employment Growth in the Context of Structural Change*[1] the view was put forward that important capital productivity gains in the communications sector have occurred. But it was further argued that for such gains to have a widespread effect throughout the economy it will be necessary to make significant advances in the design and development of other types of capital goods, such as robots, sensors, process control instrumentation, and so forth. There is some evidence of parallel gains in these areas too but for the potential benefits to be realised, an enormous wave of technical change will be needed in sectors far removed from the electronics and communications industries. This, it was argued, is predicated upon change in major social institutions, including education and training, but also throughout the work and decision-making process. Even now when unemployment is high, persistent skill shortages are found, particularly in electronic engineering, software design and systems analysis, and people are working with technologies at all levels, including management, for which they are inadequately prepared and trained.

These considerations put a different perspective upon the usual way that the "optimistic" versus "pessimistic" controversies of the employment effects of new technologies are conducted, where it seems to be assumed that technological development will happen exogenously and will then have fixed employment consequences. The above argument places the responsibility both for technological advance and its uses throughout the economy, upon the decisions and organisation of human society. The implications for education and training thus extend well beyond the preparation of workers with the new skills needed to use this technology. It implies the much broader education of society to be able to use technology to the ends it chooses, and to innovate and create in order to harness its potential. It also means, conversely, educating society so that new technologies do not further ends that are undesired. This responsibility not only rests with formal education institutions, but it is inconceivable that such large-scale change could occur without a prominent role being played by education and training systems. In emphasizing the dislocations, shortages and inadequate preparation that *presently* exist, the perspective is also altered from one that essentially addresses the future. The challenges for education to promote innovation, creativity, and changes in the formation of knowledge and skills are contemporary, not just long term.

Seen in this light, predictions of the implications of technological development for levels of skill requirements throughout economies generally are hazardous – precisely because they are not exogenous and inevitable. That widespread *change* in the skills used and required in the economy will occur is widely recognised. But, as with prognoses of the future levels of employment under the impact of technological change, views differ widely about the nature of employment in the years to come. Some argue that as technology becomes more sophisticated, so will it require more highly skilled people in order to operate equipment and put it to its most productive use. Others hold an image of future developments quite at variance. They envisage that a minority of the workforce will be confronted with complex tasks, particularly managerial and technical staffs, but that many more will be in work that is unchallenging as advanced machines take over intellectual work functions at present in human hands (e.g. of co-ordination, monitoring and product control). When this view of "de-skilling"[23] is combined with the pessimistic view of the employment effects of new technologies, the picture painted of the future is not a rosy one.

Following the reasoning of the above arguments, the future is not only unknown but unknowable since the path that will be pursued depends crucially upon the ability of society and its institutions to change, and of education systems, in particular, to promote that change. Yet the fact that the "pessimistic" views are consistent with certain of the developments outlined in the section on changes in employment structures, characterised as signs of an emerging "dual" economy, warns against complacency. Even the official Department of Labor manpower projections in the United States foresee a relatively small growth of jobs for computer systems analysts, data-processing machine mechanics, and computer programmers compared with several semi- and unskilled occupations in the service sector. The urgency of a concerted educational response is thus underlined. In any event, both skills and occupations will be subject to significant change with obsolescence and skill shortages that have immediate implications for training and retraining needs.

Mention has already been made of the special training needs of manpower with middle-level skills. Broadly, this can be characterised as people with training below that normally obtained in universities and above that obtained through traditional skill training, and covers such work as that done by paraprofessionals, technologists and technicians, functions which combine technical and managerial responsibility. Such people have to keep abreast of changes in scientific and technical knowledge and ensure that they are transformed into the action needed to produce goods and services. Their education and training call for concerted policies by educational institutions, particularly non-university tertiary colleges, and new kinds of courses and curricula that integrate theoretical and practical learning, introduce new pedagogical approaches and construct closer links with local economic activities.

One aspect of technological development meriting special attention for education and training concerns the changing nature of work organisation, that is, the social and technical features that govern the utilisation of human resources. There are many signs that technological innovations have increased the importance of working in groups. This can mean simply the greater interdependence of one worker with another as productive or administrative processes become more closely interconnected. Or it may be more far-reaching, requiring that each worker can understand and perform the functions of each other person working collectively with them. For education and training, this implies that a wider range, or polyvalence, of knowledge and skills will be needed, and not preparation in a specific set of occupational skills corresponding to a single job title. The more general, less tangible challenge to education may be more important, however: how to promote the ability to learn and work collectively, which will mean a significant departure, in method and approach, from the competitive, individualised educational philosophy which often typifies the formal system.

In sum, the consequences of technological and employment change affect education and training in many ways, from the most general to the highly concrete. Educating for and about technological change as part of a broad social awareness of its use and effects will critically involve the formal education system as well as other agencies and institutions. The promotion of creativity and innovation throughout the economy has a significant educational component. The revision of the content of education and concepts of literacy, so that they take full account of the "new languages of modernity", embracing computer and technological "literacy" (see Chapter 5), is a generalised educational task. Concrete revisions of training and retraining opportunities so that existing skill shortages can be reduced or removed, and so that young people are not trained with skills that are already out-dated or obsolescent, are required no less than training to relocate workers whose jobs disappear with "labour-saving" technological investments and thus ensure that adults are not by-passed by technological innovation.

NOTES AND REFERENCES

1. *Employment Growth and Structural Change,* OECD, Paris, 1985.
2. "The Role of Education and Training in Relation to the Employment and Unemployment of Young People", Statement by the Education Committee, OECD, Paris, 1983 (document for general distribution).
3. See *Recurrent Education: A Strategy for Lifelong Learning,* OECD/CERI, Paris, 1973.
4. *Policy Conference on Economic Growth and Investment in Education,* (held in Washington D.C., 16-20 October 1961) OECD, Paris, 1966.
5. Early influential statements being T. Schultz's "Investment in Human Capital", in *American Economic Review,* March 1961; and G.S. Becker's *Human Capital,* National Bureau of Economic Research, New York, 1964.
6. See E.F. Denison, *Why Growth Rates Differ,* The Brookings Institution, Washington D.C., 1967.
7. e.g. H.S. Parnes, *Forecasting Educational Needs for Economic and Social Development,* OECD, Paris, 1962.
8. On some of the problems of manpower forecasting, see *The Future of Vocational Education and Training,* OECD, Paris, 1983.
9. L. Thurow, *Generating Inequality,* Basic Books, New York, 1975.
10. See R. Edwards *et al.* (eds.), *Labour Market Segmentation,* Heath, Lexington, Mass., 1975.
11. *OECD Employment Outlook,* OECD, Paris, September 1983, p. 63.
12. K. Arrow, "Education as a Filter", in *Journal of Political Economy,* July 1973.
13. I. Berg, *Education and Jobs: The Great Training Robbery,* Beacon Press, Boston, 1971.
14. R. Rumberger, "The Job Market for College Graduates 1960-1990", Project Report No. 83-A3; Institute for Research on School Finance and Governance, Stanford University, February 1983, Table 2.
15. *OECD Employment Outlook, op. cit.,* pp. 51-52.
16. *OECD Employment Outlook, op. cit.,* p. 52.
17. *The Integration of Women into the Economy,* OECD, Paris (forthcoming), Chapter II.
18. *The Employment and Unemployment of Women in OECD Countries,* OECD, Paris, 1984.
19. *OECD Employment Outlook, op. cit.,* p. 67.
20. Referred to in *Le Monde* of 15th January 1984.
21. See "Report on Vocational Education", OECD, Paris, 1980 (document for general distribution); and *The Future of Vocational Education and Training,* OECD, Paris, 1983.
22. "Employment Prospects for Higher Education Graduates", Paper to the Intergovernmental Conference on Policies for Higher Education in the 1980s, 12th-14th October 1981, OECD, Paris (document for general distribution).
23. For a recent discussion see H. Levin and R. Rumberger, *The Educational Implications of High Technology,* Institute for Research on School Finance and Governance, Stanford University, 1983.

Chapter 4

EDUCATIONAL EQUALITY AND THE REDISTRIBUTION OF SOCIAL OPPORTUNITIES

CERTAIN KEY ISSUES AND APPROACHES TOWARDS EQUALITY OF OPPORTUNITY

One of the most awkward and pressing facts in education today is that there is still a substantial minority of young people who leave the school system without even the basic equipment of knowledge and skills that education imparts and which are prerequisites of modern life. Such is its importance that Chapter 6, which examines issues confronting the compulsory school in OECD countries, takes this as one of its main problematics. A central task for education remains the realisation of greater equality of opportunity especially when substantial numbers of young people come out of education inadequately prepared for modern life while increasing numbers of others are introduced to the most advanced and complex forms of knowledge and skills.

No easy formulas exist for removing educational "failure", which is rendered especially difficult because it is a "moving target" rather than a static one. It is a moving target in an absolute sense because the demands and requirements of modern life increase as societies become more complex. What might have been adequate preparation in knowledge and skills several decades ago is now scarcely sufficient. It is a moving target in a relative sense because, short of achieving absolute uniformity in educational attainment, there will always be some who are below the rest. Indeed, in this respect organised education can be regarded as a victim of its own success. The fact that educational progress has been marked during the twentieth century with so many now enjoying extensive educational careers, highlights the position of those at the bottom of the educational ladder. Schools and colleges are able, as is their responsibility, to seek to improve the accomplishments and interests of students in absolute terms. Much more intractable is that their very success in doing so threatens to push the least advantaged educationally still further behind.

The roots of the inequalities that are manifest in classrooms, schools and colleges extend, however, well beyond the education system and into the society and economy around it. It is now universally recognised that there are severe constraints on the ability of education systems to equalise achievements and opportunities, given the powerful socio-economic influences that serve to reinforce them. The social patterning of success and failure in schools and colleges is universal. In all Member countries, those who come from less privileged backgrounds, from the poor areas of city and countryside, from many ethnic and cultural minorities, are numerous among the least successful in education. The existence of these social inequalities importantly shapes the way that the objective of equality of educational opportunity should be interpreted. It is a goal that should always inspire educational policy even though it can never be fully realised. Some have wrongly interpreted the constant existence of educational inequalities in OECD countries as evidence either that previous educational policies have failed or that equality goals should be abandoned. Neither is true. It is evidence, rather, of the need for further and renewed application to an urgent and necessarily unfinished task.

Educational attainment is thus importantly shaped by the social origins and milieux of the students. In turn, it is powerfully associated with their eventual social and economic destinations – the jobs, the incomes and, more generally, the life-chances that follow after students leave the education system. Youth unemployment and the difficulties many young people have of getting a foothold in the labour market, which may well have ineradicable repercussions throughout the lives of those affected, make this especially serious. The young unemployed are heavily concentrated among schools' low-achievers. As discussed in the previous chapter, education cannot be expected to solve these major employment problems whose root causes are economic. Yet neither can it abandon its responsibility to improve the prospects of the least advantaged, especially because the education system sorts and selects so decidedly a sizeable number of young people for an uncertain and marginal future. The starting point for tackling these questions has, however, to be modified from the one that typified much of the optimistic discussion of the "Golden Years" of education. Then, in a world of economic growth and seemingly ever-expanding labour market opportunities, the emphasis was upon allowing greater equality of access to the more prestigious educational establishments and experiences. The hope was that less advantaged social groups would then enjoy readier access to the more rewarded and rewarding rungs of society that previously had been predominantly the reserve of their more privileged contemporaries. "Access to advantage" summarises this laudable aim.

Not all shared the expectation of widespread upward social mobility, even at the time. There were those who were at pains to point out that, even were educational reform suddenly successful in reducing social differences in educational attainment, the extent of actual upward social movement would necessarily be limited because those originating from the top can move nowhere but down if they are mobile, and because there is much less room in the upper echelons than on the lower rungs[1]. Nonetheless, with working-class participation in the higher reaches of education systems so disproportional to their numbers, these theoretical limitations could be seen as churlishly academic.

Economic recession, unemployment and depressed labour market opportunities now make the "access to advantage" aspiration alone insufficient. It remains important to aim to ensure fairer chances of access to a good education and to well-paid, rewarding jobs. But when such jobs become scarce, and unemployment widespread, it becomes more necessary to focus upon the other end of the socio-economic spectrum. This is not to expect educational panaceas. Rather, it is a question of political will and commitment – a commitment to ensure that the disadvantaged are a policy priority and do not fall further behind.

This is no easy challenge. For one of the "iron laws" of educational development is that privileged groups and social strata constantly seek to maintain that privilege. When structures and institutions are made more open, the expectation of greater equality of educational chances has frequently been disappointed by the ability of the better-off to establish new criteria of success and by strategies that sidestep equalising policies. The right of parents to seek what is perceived to be the best education for their children cannot be denied. But it further underlines the need for commitment to those who do not enjoy the same privilege as others.

One significant factor that has altered the way this commitment is approached has been the emergence into the policy arena in the last decade or more of groups or sections of the population with a greater awareness of their own identity and interests in educational matters. This includes girls and women, the handicapped, cultural or ethnic groups and those of particular geographical locations, and in each case there has been more conscious recognition of the validity of their special needs and claims. Thus, a single dimension along which equality and inequality can be measured is less readily applicable and this limits the usefulness of general formulations and concepts of equality as against more concrete, targeted measures.

One result of these changes is that educational policy concerning disadvantage is now more likely to be discussed in the concrete terms of specific problems – such as the educational problems of inner cities or the young unemployed – or of disadvantaged groups. The advantage with the more concrete perspectives is that they directly focus on real-world problems, though it risks the neglect of a more general understanding of social disadvantage in education systems.

In the following section, some of the main features of the evolving position of the less advantaged groups in education will be outlined. As discussed above, the focus can be either upon the degree to which the higher reaches of education systems have opened up to those who traditionally have been under-represented or upon the situation of those at the other end of the spectrum. Findings from both perspectives are presented, as well as special consideration of the position of girls and women and of the children of migrants in contemporary education systems.

DISADVANTAGED GROUPS IN EDUCATION

The Educational Situation of the Less Advantaged

Access to higher levels of education

Pessimism concerning the lack of progress in the access of lower socio-economic students to higher levels of education is widespread, almost fashionable. But the findings upon which this pessimism is based need to be put in perspective. The educational expansion of recent decades has meant that many more students from poorer backgrounds have enjoyed further and higher education than their mothers and fathers did only a generation before. This is a genuine achievement of post-war educational policies.

The speed of progress and the actual numbers involved have naturally varied from country to country, influenced by such factors as the institutional structure in place in each, and the degree to which less privileged students have historically been enabled to continue in education. It is often argued that, while absolute gains have been made, progress in relative terms of the low socio-economic status (SES) student towards the *baccalauréat* or the university degree has been negligible. But this is unduly pessimistic and belittles the scale of educational change that has taken place – as several examples illustrate. In Norway, only 3.5 per cent of pupils from manual working background achieved the matriculation examination at the end of upper secondary schooling in the beginning of the 1950s. Less than thirty years later, this had increased several-fold to 20.8 per cent[2]. For the comparable baccaulauréat qualification in France, only 2.5 per cent of workers' children achieved it in 1962 compared with nearly 11 per cent by 1976[3]. Two examples for higher education are no less striking. Only 6.5 per cent of German university students beginning their studies as recently as 1966 had fathers who were manual workers. In a mere decade, this had more than doubled to 15.9 per cent by 1976[4]. An approximate doubling of the working-class proportion among higher education students also took place in Denmark over the last thirty years or so from around 9 per cent to about 17 per cent today[5].

Important though these advances are, they have to be qualified by a number of significant countervailing and less positive factors. Despite the widening of educational access to less privileged students, the disparities in educational success and failure between the upper and lower strata remain very marked[6]. Many more university students are still drawn from middle-class backgrounds just as the early school leaver tends disproportionately to be of working-class origin or a second-generation migrant or of a cultural minority. Moreover, even if the rate of increase of the less advantaged students in the higher levels of education may have been greater than that of their more privileged contemporaries, in terms of actual numbers of students, it has often been less. On this question, a study in the United Kingdom concluded from a survey of class inequalities thus:

"In summary, school inequalities of opportunity have been remarkably stable over the forty years which our study covers. Throughout, the service [upper] class has had roughly three times the chance of the working-class of getting some kind of selective secondary schooling. Only at 16 has there been any significant reduction in relative class chances, but even here the absolute gains have been greater for the service class"[7].

The difference between rates of growth and increases in actual numbers of the different social groups in education is well illustrated by analysis of the French baccalauréat results[8]. The proportion of workers' children achieving the baccalauréat grew well over sixfold from 5 761 to 38 243 between 1962 and 1976 – a growth of numbers of over 32 000. Those who achieved the baccalauréat whose background was higher and middle management and the professions grew from 26 093 in 1962 to 76 235 in 1976 – a threefold increase only but a significantly higher growth in absolute numbers of over 50 000. These examples serve to underline that the general educational expansion of recent decades benefited all groups, and not only the less favoured in society.

A second major qualification is the observation that since the mid-1970s there appears to have been a halt or even a reversal in the progress that had been seen in the preceding years in some countries. Norwegian and Swedish data both point in this direction. The same Norwegian study that charted substantial working-class increases in success in the matriculation examination between 1951 and 1978 also describes how much of this took place in the period 1963 to 1974 with "no clear tendencies towards more equality either before 1963 or after 1974"[9]. Despite the many policies in Sweden to promote equality of opportunity, the long-standing trend towards more equal social representation in universities slowed down in the last decade and may have even reversed by the end of the 1970s[10]. And Germany, having experienced the sharp increase in working-class representation in universities over the decade 1966-1976, as mentioned above, has enjoyed less certain progress since then. The proportion of 15.9 per cent new university students being workers' children in 1976 fell to a slightly lower level for each of the subsequent four years and the latest available figure (1980) is 14.7 per cent[11].

The social patterns of university enrolments in the United Kingdom appear to have followed this reversal more sharply still. It has even been suggested:

"The university data suggest that participation by the children of manual workers improved, albeit slowly, in the post-war period up to around 1970 and then declined until by 1978 it appears to have fallen below the pre-war level"[12].

Data from the Norwegian study suggest that among those who achieve the matriculation examination (a number which has grown markedly over the post-war period), the social gap for those who go on to university has increased over this period, not decreased[13], and there is some evidence of this from Japan[14]. It is illustration again that whereas greater numbers of the less privileged have gained access to these more prestigious educational levels and institutions with expansion, the more privileged students have also taken advantage of the opening of opportunities. At the same time, progress towards greater equalisation seems to have slowed, faltered or even reversed since the early 1970s[15].

The third main qualification to the conclusion of greater participation of lower socio-economic classes in the higher reaches of education systems is that it may be misleading to compare levels of enrolment in the 1950s or 1960s with the 1980s since it is not to compare "like with like". With the expansion of universities, for example, it may well be that university attendance itself means something different from when it was the more exclusive and select experience of the élite. One element of this is the reduced power of the degree to assure its holder a good job or high income in the labour market with the "devaluation" of educational credentials. Another element is the quality of the educational resources and learning experiences available to students throughout a much expanded system. As discussed in more detail in Chapter 8, the internal hierarchy of programmes has sharpened over recent years. It follows that it may well have become more meaningful to review the position of less advantaged groups in the more prestigious, sought-after programmes if comparison is to be made with the period before mass higher education.

Examples from a number of countries suggest that progress towards greater access for the less advantaged student in the more prestigious programmes has not matched their overall representation. Sons and daughters of manual workers in universities in France made up slightly more than 13 per cent of all students in 1979-80. However, they were only 7.5 per cent of students in medicine, 7.2 per cent of those studying pharmacy and only 6.5 per cent in dentistry, these being the selective, prestigious faculties. The sons and daughters of professional and higher-level managers comprised nearly half the students in these faculties, being thus clearly over-represented since about a third of university students originated from these social categories (which is considerably higher than their numbers in the population as a whole)[16]. A review of studies in Australia describes the consistent pattern of faculties of medicine and law drawing heavily on higher SES students compared with education students who have the smallest proportion of fathers from professional and managerial positions[17]. A Swedish study[18] summarises a very similar picture:

"There are, however, clear differences even among individuals who have completed an academic degree as regards the different groups. Those who come from lower social classes have generally chosen to study at the faculties of arts and sciences. Individuals from higher social classes, on the other hand, often choose programmes which take longer to complete and are more expensive, but which lead to professions with higher status and incomes, such as those of physician, dentist and veterinarian." (p. 83).

It is a recurring finding that the faculties and programmes that have made the greatest strides in opening their doors to the non-traditional student are those which the better-off increasingly tend to avoid in favour of those that offer greater opportunities in subsequent employment. These more open faculties tend also to risk most cutbacks in staff and resources (see Chapter 8).

The other end of the spectrum: educational and social disadvantage

The education system can be likened to a difficult obstacle race – students compete against each other, some are sufficiently favoured or talented to keep up, while others drop behind or drop out altogether, numerous hurdles are present that many do not cross or which define an alternative track and perhaps exit. Survival in the race is a premium. Much of the sorting and selection takes place before the students attain the later stages of the education system. Inequalities in higher education result largely from decisions taken earlier in the educational process. Indeed, if the lower SES student has survived in the education system as far as the end of academic upper secondary level, his or her chances of continuing on to higher education are often not much lower than those of their more advantaged classmates[19]. But many more of the less advantaged will have already been eliminated from the race, especially at one of the major hurdles such as the passage from compulsory to post-compulsory schooling.

Educational policies designed to tilt the balance in favour of the less advantaged student run up against the "iron law" mentioned above – of the privileged maintaining, through initial advantage or deliberate strategy, their advantage in education. Thus, the widespread adoption of comprehensive systems of secondary schooling has not eliminated inequalities of opportunity as some had hoped, and in some respect the removal of differentiated institutional structures, in rendering the selection process more implicit, may not have made it any easier to eliminate. In part, it is a matter of deliberate strategy by the better-off – for example, by moving to neighbourhoods that are regarded as having good schools, thereby exacerbating the social contrast of schools in one district compared with another and circumventing the equalising effect that a system of comprehensive schools seeks to realise. But more generally, it is clear that the process of selection is much more deep-seated than that imposed by the institutional structure of schools. The OECD report on compulsory schooling[20] concluded:

> "It might thus be inferred that there is a clear-cut split among and within OECD countries over whether or not to offer common compulsory schooling for all. In practice, however, there exists the more fundamental crux as to how much differentiation there is *within* schools and at what age it begins. For so-called common schools can vary enormously in the way they distribute pupils in groups and classes and apply the curriculum." (p. 23)

Taking it further still, whatever the actual distribution of time, staff, resources, and subjects within the school, the learning process is one that the advantaged child, with the appropriate cultural capital, can readily profit from. Indeed, "progressive" pedagogies that aim to extend interest and discovery to all children, whatever their background, may well favour most those who bring to it the maximum capability of flourishing in the relative freedom of this kind of learning situation[21]. It is often the middle-class child, in other words, who profits most from the open classroom, discovery and individualised methods and self-directed learning.

Yet this does not imply the pessimistic conclusion that "schools make no difference". This expression of scepticism about the effects of schooling was encouraged by American studies that purported to show that schools themselves played a relatively minor role in the reproduction of social and economic inequalities[22] or that compensatory educational programmes could show little for the expenditures involved. But studies such as Jencks's raised more questions than they provided firm answers and the methodology used was seriously questioned, even at the time. Subsequent evaluations of the enduring effects of early compensatory interventions on later educational achievements have shown definite results and long-term improvement in school attainments. The conclusion "schools make no difference" is, in any case, highly partial both because the criteria used to assess this have covered only a small range of educational aims and because the analyses themselves have yielded equivocal results.

This is not to underestimate the difficulty confronting educational policy in improving the position of the least advantaged. Not only are the more advantaged better placed to profit from available opportunities and actively seek to maintain that advantage. But educational policy is caught in the dilemma of attempting to extend opportunities and qualifications to as many youngsters as possible, but in the process leaving those who do not succeed further behind still. The broadening of access to education, and the degree to which the least successful can accordingly be easily identified, may mean that education systems are actually serving to make initial disadvantage more determinate and difficult to escape. The solution for them cannot thus be measures and policies that merely prolong education, extending the obstacle race by providing "more of the same".

The Educational Situation of Girls and Women

Interest in and concern about the situation of girls and women in education have grown considerably over the 1970s and 1980s. Stimulated by the general movement for equality between the sexes, and the evolving position of women which is one of the great social changes of our time, much attention has come to be given to inequalities of opportunity of education and training between girls and boys, men and women. In this regard, education is seen both as important in itself, since access to knowledge and learning is an accepted right in modern societies, and as strategic to the achievement of greater equality in the other economic, social and domestic spheres.

Many choose to emphasize the degree to which girls and women continue to suffer from educational disadvantage compared with boys and men. Particularly in terms of the rigid divisions by sex in the subjects studied and types of education and training pursued, this is justified. But overemphasis upon female disadvantage can be misleading and hinder the cause of promoting greater equality between the sexes in education since the evidence[23] shows real progress towards a more even balance between girls and boys, women and men, albeit varying between countries and between types of education and training. In all sectors, particularly in upper secondary education but in higher education too, greater equality has been achieved. In many countries, more boys than girls now leave education with no school qualifications. Except at the most advanced educational levels, the attainment of boys is often lower. Girls and women are not everywhere, therefore, at a disadvantage. This progress should be fully recognised for the fact that many girls and women are now pursuing extensive educational careers, and in areas once almost exclusively "male", demonstrates that the patterns of educational attainment visible at any one time are not fixed by natural, biological limits. Both the extent of change over time within countries, and the differences between countries in the extent to which traditionally male and female preserves have been modified or broken down, show that change has been, and is, possible.

However, while progress has been made, crucial female disadvantage remains. The rigidity of the division into male-dominated and female-dominated subjects has changed noticeably less than overall participation rates in most OECD countries. At the compulsory level, when choice between subjects and specialisation begins, this is apparent and it becomes marked at the post-compulsory and higher levels of education. There remains significant female under-representation in scientific and technical subjects, even if there are signs of slow progress in some places. Fewer girls than boys pursue the vocational lines of study and, when they do, they tend to be concentrated into a small number of "female" branches. Very few young women are in apprenticeships. The same patterns persist for older adults, where women are well represented in general courses but are many fewer in those with a more professional orientation. The female disadvantage here is thus a dual one. First, their education is more narrowly concentrated into a limited range of subjects and options. And, secondly, the courses in which girls and women are under-represented are those with greater utility and application in the labour market. With unemployment high and job markets difficult everywhere, these are serious disadvantages. Moreover, women are still a minority of university students in most countries, and are significantly under-represented at the post-graduate level in all.

The factors that lie behind these patterns and inequalities are manifold and complex. Some place emphasis upon the potential of the school, and teachers in particular, to change attitudes held by girls and boys towards school subjects and attainment with the aim of encouraging girls into non-traditional fields. Attitudes are certainly a crucial element in the complex compound, but they are far from superficial. They reflect the influence that parents, the family, peers and the wider society, as well as schools, constantly exercise from the earliest moments of childhood. Nor are attitudes the only element involved. Abilities themselves are a reflection of these various and profound influences – girls develop certain abilities and boys others throughout their upbringing. Actual inequalities of opportunity, in education, training and the labour market are, equally, a crucial element that will not simply disappear with revised attitudes towards school subjects and vocational fields. And, as a further element in the compound, there is the ubiquitous influence of the norms and conventions concerning the role of the sexes in economic, social and domestic life, reinforced and reproduced through a myriad of mechanisms that provide the context and backcloth against which education and training operates. These elements are all at play and are all intricately interactive.

This discussion has focused upon the educational situation of girls and women in general. Yet, there is evidence to suggest that the advances that have been realised are concentrated among those from more privileged social strata. The factors of gender and social class interact so that to be a girl and of working-class origin means that a dual educational handicap has to be overcome. The Norwegian study summarises this dual handicap:

"... Both during transition from compulsory school and schools for secondary education as well as between matriculation exam and further education, girls are taking less advantage of their educational opportunities than boys. This tendency is much more significant in the lowest socio-economic groups"[24].

In contrast to women in higher social groups, reports a Swedish study, "the daughters of working-class parents have been almost totally unable to achieve a place in the male-dominated, high prestige programmes"[25]. The difference in the gap between men and women from different social backgrounds who have attended university in Australia confirms the same picture. About 30 per cent of sons of professionals study at university compared with about a quarter of daughters of comparable social milieu. The sons of semi- and unskilled workers are well behind their more privileged fellows – only some 5 per cent have studied at this level, a sixth of the rate for professionals' sons. But for girls, the size of the gap in the rates of university attendance is double since only 2 per cent of the daughters of semi- and unskilled workers had managed to reach this level in the education system[26].

Certain groups of girls and women thus face particular difficulties in the education system. The dual handicap of being a female and of low SES background triples if she is also the daughter of one of the many groups of migrants that live in OECD countries. It is the position of migrants' children that is considered next.

The Educational Situation of Migrants

The educational disadvantage of young migrants is a special cause for concern in a number of OECD countries. The school career of the vast majority of young migrants attending schools in the host country is short and ends without a diploma. They are increasingly numerous in secondary education, where they take the short cycle preparing for rapid entry to the labour market without any special skills. Compared with the education of young nationals, the school career of young foreigners is seldom normal and the disparities between the situation of national and foreign pupils in education systems are persisting and are liable to increase.

Migrants' children, like those of many cultural minorities in OECD countries, suffer the standard features of educational under-achievement. Many fall behind in their schooling and some do not attend school at all. A French enquiry, for example, showed that while 27 per cent of young nationals are behind in primary school, this figure rose to 49 per cent for young foreigners[27]. A higher-than-average proportion is to be found in special education. Two examples illustrate this tendency. In Switzerland in 1981/82 less than 7 per cent of young nationals were in special classes at primary level compared with 11 per cent of foreigners. The comparable figures for Luxembourg were 3.3 per cent and 7.9 per cent. It is implausible that these gaps can be explained by different levels of handicap suggesting that linguistic difficulties are the real reason. This raises serious questions about the use and nature of special education as well as the consequences of being outside mainstream provision.

Many young foreigners and migrants are oriented also to short-cycle vocational branches and are early school-leavers. The respective percentages of nationals and foreigners in the branches of short-cycle secondary education in 1981/82 were 42.1 and 51.8 in Germany, 61.2 and 79.4 in Luxembourg, 36.1 and 46.3 in Switzerland. In 1980/81, the same proportions were 43.8 per cent and 68.6 per cent in Belgium, 18.5 per cent and 29.4 per cent in France. Relatively few make it to the longer cycles and higher levels of the education system[28]. Throughout, average achievement levels are low.

Part of the problem is recognised to be the frequent inadequate mastery of the language of the host country. Several studies have shown, as might be expected, that the longer the pupil or student has lived in the host country, the less important do linguistic difficulties become. Policy initiatives have placed particular emphasis on the linguistic factor and much can be done in this domain, particularly initially. However, the problems also reside in the fact that the socio-economic situation of migrants is so low. It is scarcely surprising that educational achievement is below average when serious problems of overcrowding, bad housing and poor amenities are frequently the norm. Indeed, some research suggests that the children of migrants perform little differently from the rest of the school population who come from identical socio-economic backgrounds. This indicates that the problems cannot be properly addressed if they are regarded as linguistic, particularly as it must be recognised that an increasing proportion of young migrants are born in the country of immigration. The educational problems of the latter cannot be seen to reside purely or even mainly in the inadequate mastery of the language of that country.

Targeted policy measures which go beyond education, and take account of the social and economic conditions in which young migrants live, deserve special attention. There exist already programmes and initiatives of this kind in several OECD countries. Their scale and coverage, however, tend to be little more than marginal compared with the problems they are meant to address. An important aspect in this is the degree to which migrants' children, and those from cultural minorities generally, are often highly concentrated in the same schools, located conspicuously in a number of districts usually in large cities. These schools are typified not only by all the problems of inadequate facilities and provision normally associated with poor districts. They have also to cope with the added and crucial dimension of classes with high levels of minority children. In addition, the staff and personnel of these schools have rarely received any special training for the problems they have to face.

Targeted measures are thus one important response, though in reaction to the more specific question of geographical concentration, re-siting represents another kind of strategy. As learned from experience with compensatory programmes for the disadvantaged, however, they are likely to bring greater success if they extend beyond the purely educational. This means involving the community as much as possible in the activities of schools. It also means that educational initiatives should be one aspect only of a range of measures and policies that address the wider economic and social problems of the community.

THE BROADER CONTEXT

Selection and Meritocracy

That education should serve economic needs and that educational qualifications do play an important role in the labour market was discussed at length in the previous chapter where both positive and negative aspects were described. The dilemma recurs that education and training systems are expected to play their full part in developing and maintaining the complex knowledge that modern economies require and yet in so doing act as such powerful mechanisms of social selection that, contrary to the aim of promoting greater social equality, they may actually reinforce it.

In responding to this dilemma, realistic account should be taken of at least two basic considerations concerning the links between education and the larger society and economy around it. First, to a greater or lesser degree, education systems always act as selection mechanisms. Recognising this does not mean that inequitable educational and social selection should be complacently accepted. Rather, the existence of selection should be faced and accounted for rather than wished away as much discussion in this field has tended to do. Secondly, social hierarchies and income inequalities are extremely resilient to change. It would be wrong to set education the over-exacting objective of erasing them altogether. Those who expected radical socio-economic transformation from school reforms alone were basing this hope on an over-demanding social theory about the relation between education and the wider society and economy around it.

In examining the links between education and the labour market, and assessing the prospects of educational change to realise a more equal distribution of life-chances, a significant development has been the "devaluation" of the occupational and income rewards associated with any particular level of certificate or qualification. In no small part it stems from the expansion of education and the proliferation of diplomas. The race after scarce rewards has become more crowded. At the same time, these rewards are now more scarce, particularly with growing unemployment[29]. The metaphor of a race, used previously to describe the education system, becomes even more appropriate when the perspective is extended to include the role of credentials in giving access to, and mobility in, the labour market.

With attention upon equality, the effect of the race for diminishing opportunities may well turn out to be more serious than a "devaluation" of educational certificates in labour

47

market terms. Not only does the cost of being educationally empty-handed go up and the expected pay-off in the labour market of a given level of qualification come down ("devaluation"), but the power of diplomas *alone* to alter the labour market chances of the individual could well be reduced. As more present themselves for vacancies or promotion with a plethora of certificates, the more do these certificates become necessary (but insufficient) screening devices for jobs. In this case, other sorts of personal and social characteristics become decisive. And the very personal and social characteristics that are likely to make up the difference between the necessary and the sufficient for labour market success – for example, styles of speech and dress, information and contacts, ambition – are precisely those where less privileged groups find themselves again at a disadvantage. The hurdles to be traversed do not, therefore, cease once the education system is left. Entry into the labour market, and the first years of establishing a career, are a continuation of the difficult obstacle race.

This implies reassessment of the extent to which OECD societies are becoming more or less meritocratic. Meritocracies can be viewed as societies where individuals' socio-economic rewards depend upon their educational attainment. A more demanding definition could be derived from Young's[30] original treatment in the 1950s – social rewards are distributed according to "IQ plus effort". More demanding still, if necessarily vague, would be that a meritocracy is where these rewards are distributed on the basis of relevant "talent".

For many, there is no essential conflict between the advocacy of greater equality of opportunity and meritocracy, the aim being to reduce the degree that an individual's rewards and life-chances depend upon his or her social background in favour of his or her own capabilities. A major argument put forward by those seeking greater equality of opportunity has been that societies would be more equitable the closer that they become a meritocracy in both the first (education) sense and the second ("IQ plus effort"), pointing out that the social biases of education distort achievement such that many from less advantaged backgrounds do not succeed in education in accordance with their measured capabilities. Even accepting this to be true, others have been less convinced that equality and meritocracy are similar and unconflicting aims. The most unequal society can be highly meritocractic depending on the criteria of social advancement. If lack of necessary educational credentials excludes the individual from reasonable labour market prospects, can the idea of meritocracy be readily embraced by those who wish to see more equal societies?

Thus we return to the question of whether societies are becoming more or less meritocratic. They could be described as becoming less meritocratic either if social and economic rewards are distributed in a more random way, or else if social background and privilege are re-emerging as more important influences upon eventual socio-economic success. That educational diplomas alone are less than sufficient, when credentials are plentiful and labour market openings scarce, to secure jobs comparable with those that others with similar levels of qualification possess, suggests that a move away from meritocracy could well characterise current trends. This is even more true if the other less tangible factors that come to play a more powerful role in labour market advancement turn out to be socially biased.

Broad Implications for Policy

The arguments of this chapter, as well as the signs of a developing "dual" economy outlined in the previous chapter, point to the conclusion that education's long-standing commitment to contribute to greater equality of opportunity is more than ever essential. However, it has also been shown that there are severe societal constraints on the ability of the education system to realise greater social equality both because of the resilience with which the already privileged protect their position and because all education systems are, to a greater or lesser degree, socially selective. In striving to realise greater educational equality, it is important to reaffirm that education is essentially the organisation of the learning experience, something that can easily be forgotten with the preoccupation with education's role as a vehicle for social mobility and the distributor of certificates. Concentrating the focus upon what is learned, and how it is learned, this pushes curricular and pedagogical issues to the fore (see Chapter 6). In this respect, "quality" and "equality", far from standing in opposition to each other, as is commonly assumed, in fact come together. Pursuit of both requires that greater attention be given to the nature of the learning process. And both require that the existing inadequacies experienced by the low-achiever – inadequacies of provision and of personal benefit – become a major priority. Far from conflicting, the goals of greater "quality" and "equality" point in identical directions.

Focusing upon education as the organisation of the learning experience is not restricted to *what* is learned, and *how*, but it also crucially concerns *when*. It is difficult to see how the finality of educational success and failure can be favourably modified without breaking into the rigid pattern of early educational experiences being so determinate of later chances in life. A major reason why international interest in lifelong learning emerged initially was the fear that a heavily "front-loaded" education system reinforces the initial advantage that the more privileged classes enjoy over the rest of the population. Continuing or recurrent education is thus an indispensable component of a general strategy for greater equality of opportunity in modern, democratic societies.

Yet, despite policy pronouncements in favour of lifelong learning, and despite developments in further and higher education in favour of "new" groups, there have been increasing pressures to keep young people within the institutionalised guardianship of education and training leading, if anything, to a strengthening of the "front-end" organisation of educational provision. That much of this has been in the vocational and training sectors has added a special twist to the process. The proliferation of short-term measures for narrow vocational preparation tends to push those who take such courses towards specific types of job and may reinforce still further the inequitable rigidities in the links between education received in the early part of the lifespan and the labour market. The very measures of a short-term and instrumental kind designed to redress labour market disadvantage run the risk of having the opposite effect. And, as discussed in the previous chapter, they may even run counter to their explicit labour market aims of fostering preparedness for, and flexibility in, the world of work. As a strategy for greater equality, recurrent education must go considerably further than simply blurring the lines between the last year of school and the first ones in the job market. It will also have to avoid the real risks of actually exacerbating social inequalities rather than ameliorating them.

For education to contribute significantly to greater social equality, whether experienced early or later in the individual's life, its role must be seen to be wider than that of provision of the qualifications to be used in working life. The social opportunities of modern societies extend well beyond the workplace and, as already discussed, the proportion of people's lifetimes spent in work is declining. For education to equip people fully to participate in modern societies and to break into the lockstep of it serving to quicken the crowded race after scarce labour market opportunities, then full emphasis should be given to its role as preparation for political participation, for cultural activity, for leisure and retirement, for community life, for health and welfare, over and above its vocational preparation mission.

NOTES AND REFERENCES

1. C.A. Anderson, "A Sceptical Note on Education and Mobility", in *American Journal of Sociology*, Vol. 66, 1961: pp. 560-570; and R. Boudon, *Education, Opportunity and Social Inequality*, J. Wiley, New York, 1974.

2. P.O. Aamodt, *Education and Social Background*, Samfunnsokonomiske Studier 51, Central Bureau of Statistics of Norway, 1982.

3. "Evolution des probabilités d'accès au baccalauréat selon la catégorie sociale d'origine 1962-1976", in *Le Baccalauréat*, Etudes et Documents 81.2., Ministère de l'Education nationale, Service des études informatiques et statistiques, 1981.

4. *Grund und Struktur Daten 1982/83*, Der Bundesminister für Bildung und Wissenschaft, Bonn, pp. 150-151.

5. E.J. Hansen, *Hvem bryder den Sociale Arv?, (Who Breaks the Social Inheritance?)*, The Danish National Institute of Social Research Publication 112, 1982, Table 15.

6. This was documented repeatedly through the end of the 1960s and into the 1970s by the OECD. See in particular: "Group Disparities in Educational Participation and Achievement", Conference on Policies for Educational Growth, OECD, Paris, 1971. T. Husén, *Social Influences on Educational Attainment*, OECD/CERI, Paris, 1975; and *Education, Inequality and Life-chances*, Vols. I and II, OECD, Paris, 1975.

7. A.H. Halsey, A.F. Heath and J.M. Ridge, *Origins and Destinations: Family, Class and Education in Modern Britain*, Clarendon Press, Oxford, 1980, p. 205.

8. "Evolution des probabilités d'accès au baccalauréat selon la catégorie sociale d'origine 1962-1976", *op. cit.*

9. P.O. Aamodt, *Education and Social Background, op. cit.*, p. 165.

10. A. Svensson, *Equality in the University: Fiction or Reality?* UHA report 1981:25.

11. *Grund und Struktur Daten 1982/83, op. cit.*, pp. 150-151.

12. M. Shattock," Demography and Social Class: The Fluctuating Demand for Higher Education in Britain" in *European Journal of Education*, Vol. 16, Nos. 3-4, 1981.

13. P.O. Aamodt, *Education and Social Background, op. cit.*, p. 166.

14. W.K. Cummings, *Education and Equality in Japan*, Princeton University Press, 1980, p. 225; though a recent Monobusho 1982 survey showed that since 1980, students from the lowest income quintile have increased their share among the university student body (18.6 per cent compared with 17.5) while the proportion from the top quintile has slightly fallen (26.6 per cent compared with 28.2 per cent).

15. Account should also be taken of the changing occupational structure of OECD countries. Blue-collar jobs have declined relative to white-collar jobs and professions, therefore leading, all other things being equal, to an expected proportional decline in working-class representation in these more prestigious levels of education. However, since these broad occupational changes have been taking place over the entire post-war period, they do not affect the conclusion that the patterns of social class recruitment have changed in the last decade.

16. *Les Etudiants: 5.2*, Statistiques des Enseignements. Tableaux et informations, Service central des statistiques, ministère de l'Education, Paris, No.14, 1981.

17. D.S. Anderson and A.E. Vervoorn. *Access to Privilege: Patterns of Participation in Australian Post-Secondary Education*, A.N.U. Press, Canberra, 1983, Chapter 9. The authors point out that teaching has traditionally been an important avenue of upward social mobility for working-class students. The severe restrictions on teacher recruitment thus frustrates one of the traditional routes for social advancement.

18. A. Svensson, "On Equality and University Education in Sweden", *in Scandinavian Journal of Educational Research*, Vol. 24, 1980.

19. See A.H. Halsey, A.F. Heath, and J.M. Ridge. *Origins and Destinations, op. cit.*, Ch. 10 and D.S. Anderson and A.E. Vervoorn, *op. cit.*, Ch. 9. In systems with very high participation levels in upper secondary education, however, entry to higher education becomes the juncture where social selection is most apparent.

20. *Compulsory Schooling in a Changing World*, OECD, Paris, 1983.

21. e.g. B. Bernstein, *Class and Pedagogies: Visible and Invisible*, CERI/OECD, Paris, 1974

22. Especially C. Jencks *et al.*, *Inequality: A Reassessment of the Effect of Family and Schooling in America*, Basic Books, New York, 1972.

23. A full review and discussion of the evidence is contained in *Educational Opportunities for Girls and Women*, OECD, Paris (forthcoming).

24. P.O. Aamodt, *Education and Social Background, op. cit.,* p. 167.

25. A. Svensson, "On Equality and University Education in Sweden", *op. cit.,* p. 84.

26. D.S. Anderson and A.E. Vervoorn, *Access to Privilege, op. cit.,* p. 147.

27. H. Bastide, *Les enfants d'immigrés et l'enseignement français,* PUF., Paris, 1982, p. 121.

28. OECD Secretariat Data.

29. For a fuller discussion see: "Re-examining Equality of Educational Opportunity", in *The OECD Observer,* March 1982.

30. M. Young, *The Rise of Meritocracy,* Thames and Hudson, London, 1958.

Chapter 5

FURTHER DIMENSIONS
OF SOCIAL AND CULTURAL CHANGE
IN THE WIDER ENVIRONMENT OF EDUCATION

THE INTERDEPENDENCE OF THE ECONOMIC, SOCIAL AND
CULTURAL DIMENSIONS OF CHANGE

The trends described in the foregoing chapters add up to a series of far-reaching social and cultural changes which shape, and which are shaped by, education. The changing labour market and educational situation of women described above, for example, is part of the global evolution of the position of women in society. Education, both in schools and later, is correctly regarded as crucial in quickening or impeding this development. The general reduction of working hours and the growth of leisure, retirement and other non-working activities, as outlined in Chapters 2 and 3, potentially carry major implications for education and its organisation and, again, all levels and sectors are affected. The mission of schools and colleges to prepare for adult life acquires a new meaning as "adult life" is typified by greater discretion to use time for personal or community activities. And the importance of recurrent education is clearly underlined as greater proportions of the week, the year and the lifetime are available for activities other than work. How far this can be used actively and creatively depends, in no small measure, upon the learning opportunities available to the adult population in each Member country.

These two examples underline how difficult, if not meaningless, it often is to separate the economic, the social and the cultural aspects of change in the wider environment of education. In few areas is this better illustrated than in seeking answers to the question: what are the major factors underlying sound economic performance? To be sure, part of the answer resides in variables regarded as strictly economic. But to a growing degree, it is recognised how much it is also an important function of the values and social institutions in place in each country. These shape significantly, if often intangibly, crucial factors such as productivity and work habits, entrepreneurial attitudes, habits of saving and patterns of consumption, attitudes to innovation and to occupational status, attitudes of consensus or conflict that underpin industrial relations. Since education is central in forming and transmitting values, it follows that its role in fostering these non-cognitive traits represents a comparable part of its impact upon the economy as its formal task of equipping the population with appropriate knowledge and skills.

VALUES

Recognition of the importance of values, and of education's role in their transmission, does not, however, provide straightforward guidelines for educational policy. Values and attitudes are learned largely through the "hidden curriculum" of schools and colleges and are, therefore, often impervious to directed change. Moreover, while changing lifestyles and social attitudes should be reflected in the offerings and organisation of educational institutions, precisely which attitudes and whose values these should be depends upon so many factors that they cannot be detailed in advance. There is the evident additional consideration of how to avoid the curriculum becoming the inculcation of ideologies or, at least, to avoid giving weight to the values of one group in society that offend those of another. The teaching of religion is historically one of the clearest examples where this question is posed, a question that has been answered in several countries by the coexistence of denominational schools with those run by the State giving parents the choice of whether they wish this to be part of the education of their children. More generally, there is fertile ground for conflicts to arise as education becomes more responsive to the community when the demands of the community take the form of very particular beliefs and values that not all share.

The responsibility of education to prepare pupils and students for adult life implies imparting an understanding of the world they will confront and it is hard to see how this can avoid attention to values and political matters. In doing so, it is critical whether political education succeeds in giving the young the means of making informed decisions about the world around them or whether values are taught and learned as facts. Controversy in this area extends even to the inclusion of the established social sciences, particularly sociology, in the school curriculum. The concern is not only one of possible ideological bias. The fear of some might actually be that the critical analysis of society and the exercise of informed interpretation and choice through greater political awareness might run directly counter to the general pedagogic climate of the classroom as well as the approach taken in other school subjects. The issue is then how far established school practices should change and how far school learning and teacher authority would be undermined by greater emphasis upon critical analysis and interpretation. Broad agreement that values are an essential component of education, therefore, does not facilitate the specific task of deciding how they should be incorporated into school life.

In relation to the subjects of the curriculum, attention to the wider context of social and cultural change and to the importance of the non-cognitive aims and outcomes of education argues for vigilance that the cultural disciplines – the arts, humanities and letters – are not downgraded at the expense of applied sciences and technical subjects in schools and colleges. The more general appreciation of ideas, and their manipulation, should be a central component of all education – for humanistic reasons, especially as more people acquire the time for greater cultural activities, but also for economic ones. The technological revolution should not be taken as indication that future needs are for advanced numeracy but impoverished literacy. The role of education in fostering perception is as important as that of developing analytical skills. Creating new links between the general and vocational in education, a principal theme in Part Three of the report, does not at all imply the neglect of certain areas of knowledge and understanding.

The dimensions and complexity of social and cultural change are many and varied and, as seen, their implications for education are not simple. In this chapter, three areas are selected for more detailed consideration that go beyond the economic focus of Chapter 3 and the equality considerations of Chapter 4: technology and the "information society", multi-culturalism, and the family and community.

THE CHALLENGE OF NEW INFORMATION TECHNOLOGIES

Many now judge that technological developments, especially in information and micro-technologies, have, now and in the future, a far-reaching impact upon every aspect of modern life[1]. Their effects upon working life, and on the nature and levels of employment, have already been discussed in Chapter 3 but arguably the impact will be much more widespread and pervasive. There are, for example, the many ways in which micro-computers can be used in the home and in the ways that information and learning can be acquired by all sections of the community outside specialised institutions. Will the book become an increasingly redundant aspect of modern life as an array of information-access technologies continue a process that the television has so forcefully begun? Will the computer replace pencil and paper both for individuals and organisations? Whatever the disagreements about the precise implications of new information technologies, it can be generally agreed that the label "information society" comes increasingly to characterise Member countries. There is consensus among specialists that the computing power available at a given purchase price is doubling about once every two years. This is clearly having far-reaching effects upon the kind of society we live in. Even more fundamental, perhaps, as far as education is concerned, is that these technologies may well be changing our models of thinking, intelligence, memory and attention and hence knowledge, learning and teaching. Thus the long-term impact upon education may extend well beyond the possibilities opened up for new ways of learning reading, writing or a foreign language.

For some, these developments represent an evolution rather than a revolution – another development, like others before, that only add to the pedagogical equipment available to schools and teachers. However, this is probably a serious underestimation of their potential as the situation is essentially new in a number of respects. First, the educational potential of the new information technologies is larger than had been anticipated two decades ago on the basis of the computer-based teaching/learning methodologies developed at the time. Developments show that they can be more than a support tool for the teacher or a new subject in curriculum. The information technologies have also the potential to change education radically in its very structure and organisation, in terms of manpower (numbers, competence profiles, task diversity, etc.) and of production and delivery systems.

But while the belief in this potential is generally shared across countries, there is a wide variety of objectives and approaches in the policies pursued both among and within countries. In some cases, new information technologies are seen as a matter affecting primarily vocational education. In others, they are seen as involving all the formal school system, including primary and pre-primary schools, and a more far-reaching approach still is to see as a matter of urgency that all citizens are involved and competent in developments that play an increasingly important part in professional and social life.

The issues raised are wide-ranging. There are relatively specific questions such as how schools should invest in equipment, the availability of different kinds of software and how education should approach the teaching of specific subjects such as information science and computing. There are the broader questions of how new information technologies can be used throughout education for new methods of learning – what are their potential and use?

However these questions are answered, it is apparent that new "languages" are part of the modern world, hence broadening the meaning and scope of "literacy". Computing skills are becoming necessary for all to acquire alongside the traditional skills of learning how to read, write and calculate. A further question is how far they should be introduced as a routine element of the school syllabus, to be learned, remembered and tested in the ordinary way. Might this not negate one of the defining and attractive characteristics of learning with the new technologies – the autonomy they allow from the ordinary routine of the classroom. It is thus necessary to consider how these "languages of modernity" should be learned in the widest terms, embracing their curricular and pedagogical implications, and those for the organisation of learning and the role of the teacher.

Chapter 4 considers in detail issues of equity and equality and they are raised in particular form in this area. Some believe that since the "languages" of computing and information science depart from the usual language and culture of teaching and the school, that are seen to embody middle-class values, attitudes and language habits, educational approaches based on new information technologies could be particularly effective in overcoming the traditional patterns of educational advantage and international disadvantage. But as described at the International CERI Conference on Education and New Information Technologies, the response of education to the technologies is already showing patterns of differential access across recipients. The dividing lines are often familiar: rich vs. poor schools, urban vs. rural establishments, vocational vs. general, secondary vs. primary education, science vs. humanities, boys vs. girls. The boundaries do not seem to be conspicuously different in higher education. The danger is already visible that efficiency could be achieved at the price of equity and equality.

Learning about modern technologies, therefore, should not be narrowly conceived to mean acquiring only the skills for their use, nor is it free of risks. Priority should be given to enlarging the understanding of their place in modern societies. Technological advances and uses are human developments, not inevitable and exogenous. Therefore, the overall aim should be education for the mastery of the enormous potential new technologies offer, which means the command of how they are to be used as much as how they can be operated. As such, educating for the "languages of modernity" is a part of the general learning of values as discussed above – at once controversial but, equally, unavoidable.

MULTI-CULTURALISM

The presence of ethnic and cultural minorities in schools is, perhaps, the most explicit case of cultural differences making themselves apparent in the education system. There is, however, a wide variety in the situation of minorities in OECD countries[2]. There are the differences of demographic fact: absolute numbers, concentration in given areas, relative numbers as part of the total population and recency of settlement. Other major differences are socio-cultural – the nature of the minority culture, how its members relate to their own tradition and to the majority society. Major questions of language – its relation to the dominant language, its currency and possible struggle for preservation – are raised for some minorities but not for others. The minority in question may or may not suffer significant socio-economic disadvantage. And for the more recent migrants and immigrants to a country, there is the additional dimension of their cultural (as well as economic) links with their country of emigration. Such is the range of these differences that generalisation about the

55

situation of minorities is impossible as is universal assessment of policies designed to respond to their needs.

Over recent years, much greater attention has been given in many OECD countries to policies of multi-culturalism. In part, it reflects the recognition within these countries that they are multi-cultural societies and that education should more directly respond to this reality. Political realism may be as important an element of this recognition as concern for the status of minority groups with fears of future social problems and potentially serious conflicts that a more active school policy of multi-culturalism might address or avert. In part, the attention is explained by the efforts of minorities themselves for greater recognition. In some cases, this is the claim that their children suffer special learning difficulties that should be rectified in order that greater equality of educational chances can be achieved – a claim that implies that additional and/or special educational resources be made available. In other cases, the concern is the preservation and safeguarding of language and culture which is seen to imply mother-tongue teaching, special and separate classes, or even schools, and in some cases, rejection of the school system altogether.

Though the policy instruments under discussion are essentially cultural and educational, questions of power and the political nature of different choices are intertwined with them. And because of this, there are no unequivocal directions for policies to pursue. School systems are frequently criticised roundly for the paucity of effort in becoming more multi-cultural. Where, on the other hand, significant measures are taken, the policies are open to the criticism that the State is exerting its dominance and imposing its designs upon minorities, with the implication that it is ultimately a strategy of assimilation. In the same vein, some argue that the greater the scale and visibility of policies for cultural minorities, the more do these groups become specially identified and isolated. This concern could be met by a thorough-going policy that places equal stress upon educating the majority about cultural diversity.

One of the major questions that arises is how far do educational policies that recognise diversity and differences run counter to the long-standing commitment to equality of opportunity. Some now interpret equality of opportunity actually to mean recognition of the right of each group equally to develop its own differences, through its language, customs, traditions, perhaps even with separate schools. But can "separate" mean "equal"? And how far will departure from the mainstream provision of the education system place minority pupils and students at an eventual greater disadvantage? It might be argued that these questions would be easier to resolve if the objectives of multi-culturalism and of minority groups were clarified. Yet the lack of clarity arises, in part, because of the dilemmas outlined above. Clarifying objectives cannot in itself solve genuine dilemmas. It can even serve to sharpen the lines of potential conflict.

EDUCATION, THE COMMUNITY, AND THE FAMILY

The possibility of new technologies being used extensively for individualised learning by people of all ages risks neglecting the vital communal function of education. Young people in schools learn far more than their formal syllabuses: they learn from each other and about others, about the world around them, and about growing up in a way that is made possible through sharing the same class with others. It is well known that many engage in adult education as much in order to meet other students as to follow a particular course. The student in higher education, who faces his or her professors and fellow students only in the large lecture hall, misses the contact and exchange that comes through more communal learning. It needs thus to be underlined that education involves far more than the simple absorption of facts and information. The effectiveness of policies for multi-culturalism equally is considerably reduced if they are not developed closely with, and through, the relevant communities. "Community" is thus a central concept for education.

Education's communal function, especially for adults, takes on special significance when a number of broad social changes are considered. Across OECD countries, the close, local community is frequently disappearing. Many live well apart from their workplace. Personal mobility has greatly expanded with the widespread ownership of transport and geographical mobility is often necessitated by the shifting loci of jobs. As more women go out to work, the more is the daily round of all family members organised around a common pattern of going out to school or work with home-based evening recreation. The suburban lifestyle is typified by individualised activities and loose contacts with all but the closest neighbours. The television absorbs vast quantities of national and individual time. This is not to lament the passing of the close-knit community – it has by no means disappeared nor should it be romanticised. But as a fact of life in many OECD countries, these changes in lifestyles make the communal nature and function of education all the more pertinent.

There are other important aspects in the relation between education and the community. Instead of looking to educational establishments to provide community bases that are disappearing from other settings, in much discussion in this field the community is taken as given and the school criticised for not being sufficiently active in establishing firm links with it. The general conclusion of both arguments – that education/community links should be strengthened – is the same, but the specific implications are not necessarily identical. The above argument concerning the potential of educational institutions themselves to become focal points of local communities addresses all educational institutions, including colleges, universities and adult education establishments as well as schools. It suggests that they should seek ways of using all their facilities, including those for sports and recreation, to benefit the locality. It suggests reassessment of the question of efficiency since the same buildings and facilities can be rendered more efficient by extending their use to a broader clientele and purpose as the experience of many countries shows. And it underlines the need for the benefits of schools and colleges to the community to be entered into the calculus of factors that are weighed in policies for closures. In several countries, for example Finland[3], a high priority is given to village schools and local institutions because of the importance attached to their role in maintaining local communities.

The argument that schools are insufficiently sensitive to the communities they serve is not always easy to assess. Communities and lifestyles change. Many children are in schools geographically well removed from their homes – one result of the extensive bussing policy in the United States, for example – rendering their local community more obscure. And, in any case, "community" embraces many meanings and definitions[4]. Its geographical boundaries can cover the small village up to what might be described as the national or even international community. It can be defined in terms of the social cohesion of a locality or else in a more particular way to describe a grouping of interests as, for example, with a professional community. What communities are, and still more, what the relevant one is for the school, is thus not always clear.

One concrete, if minimal, specification of the school's community are the parents. How to ensure that parents are able to have access to teachers and to the school in order that they can better understand and contribute to their children's education and in order that teachers can more fully appreciate the background of the pupils in their charge? And what are the possibilities for parents to become more fully integrated in the actual running and decision-making of the school? These questions arise from a concern that the professional activities and decisions of teachers and administrators should be open to, and influenced by, their clientele. The call for greater community and parental involvement in education is one expression of the common desire for greater accountability of the school[5]. These questions arise also because of the recognised importance played by the family, and the attitudes and support of parents specifically, in learning and educational attainment.

Although the child has many educators and effective educational policies must deal with all of them, educational policies have been primarily concerned with the institutionalised aspects of education, i.e. school education, out-of-school education, on-the-job training and education. Now there is growing interest in the educational role of the family, in particular that of parents. Popular recognition of the educational influence of the family into which the child is born is substantiated by research repeatedly showing that the family, among all the agencies of the community, continues to have much the greatest impact on the education of the young. However, since children also grow up in the schools and in the community as a whole, it is important to clarify the respective functions of each partner in the education of the young. In so doing, account needs to be taken of the different kinds of family that children are raised in, which includes special consideration of the growing numbers of single-parent families.

Yet, though the case for greater parental and community involvement is a convincing one, it does not mean that the issues raised are straightforward nor without unintended additional consequences. Compensatory programmes for the disadvantaged, for example, have been crucially based upon the recognised need to strengthen the links of the triangle – school/parents/community. But the example serves to underline that it is in advantaged areas where these links are presently strongest. How, therefore, to avoid that strengthening the ties between the school and the community will reproduce more closely still the same social differences among schools that exist among communities? And how to ensure that it is not simply the middle-class parent who profits from opportunities to influence school policy? There is the additional concern that extending widely the mechanisms for participation in the school's affairs will greatly increase the burden of bureaucracy and may actually reduce the scope for the very innovation it is intended to realise.

These issues are all implicated in the reactions to the various schemes for educational *vouchers*. The principal aim of voucher systems is to enhance parental choice of school with financial revenues distributed through a system of vouchers, with more going to schools in high demand and less to the not-so-popular. The competition so engendered, so its advocates argue, would not only increase choice and involvement of parents in the school's affairs but would also enhance efficiency and quality. The advocates comprise an unusual alliance of the political right and left, while the opponents of vouchers have long maintained that it would merely add to the problems of hard-pressed schools (which cannot be held to blame for most of their problems), would exacerbate inequalities, and produce administrative chaos. Despite the prominence that vouchers have received in academic discussion, their failure to make progress as concrete policies demonstrates that these are indeed perceived as major drawbacks.

Vouchers are one way that parental and community involvement could be extended, largely through the exercise of choice among existing publicly-administered schools. More direct, far-reaching involvement is implied where alternative, community schools are established. Countries differ considerably in the degree to which alternative schools are accommodated as part of the range of learning opportunities for young people and what "alternative school" means also differs widely among countries. In some, significant departure from the principle of publicly-provided and administered schools is anathema. Elsewhere, there has been much interest in greater community involvement through alternative schools as in the United States or in Denmark which has a flourishing "alternative" school sector with generous subsidies from the State for those who meet stipulated standards.

The degree to which these schools more closely respond to community needs thus varies and their status is related to that of the private sector more generally in each country. In countries with a large number of private schools, of which a high proportion are denominational as in France or the Netherlands, it might appear that they should be considered as clear alternatives to the public system which give expression to distinct bodies of interest in the community. But this can be misleading. In some countries they receive high levels of public financial support (in France, for example, teachers' salaries are paid by the State, where there is the appropriate contractual arrangement, as well as operating costs in secondary schools equal to levels in the public sector). And what they offer is often very similar to what is available in public schools.

There is no one relation between education and the community. At the extreme, it can be said that it covers all of the contacts and links with bodies, interests and needs external to educational establishments. In this respect, some of the most innovative and closest links with the community have developed in post-compulsory and post-secondary education; for example, in the many schemes that involve enterprises and local labour market bodies. More detailed discussion of these areas of development is given in Chapters 7 and 8.

NOTES AND REFERENCES

1. As extensively discussed at the CERI International Conference on *Education and New Information Technologies* held at OECD headquarters in Paris, 9th-12th July 1984.
2. *The Education of Minority Groups,* OECD/CERI, Gower Press, Aldershot, 1983.
3. *Reviews of National Policies for Education: Finland,* OECD, Paris, 1982.
4. See *The University and the Community: The Problems of Changing Relationships.* OECD/CERI, Paris, 1982, Chapter 3; and *School and Community,* OECD/CERI, Paris, 1975.
5. *Compulsory Schooling in a Changing World,* OECD, Paris, 1983, Chapter X.

Part Three

EDUCATIONAL RESPONSES IN THE EIGHTIES

Chapter 6

THE CHALLENGE TO COMPULSORY SCHOOLING[1]

PRESSURES ON THE COMPULSORY SCHOOL

The compulsory school system, the vast enterprise which is at the base of the educational pyramid, is currently receiving a great deal of attention in OECD countries. Demands on schools are greater than ever before and the public has taken to raising fundamental questions about their contemporary value. Are they using their extensive resources effectively? Is the learning that pupils acquire adequate and appropriate to the modern era? Are schools coping satisfactorily with the wide range of talents and interests among their pupils? Are they offering a good education to all sections of the population?

In some countries, critics even allege that educational standards have fallen in recent times, that far from bringing about greater equality of educational opportunity, would-be progressive reforms have led to an increase in inequality, that too many young people are leaving school unable to adapt to the tasks of adult life, and especially to the world of work, and that the quality and competence of the teaching force have declined. Such allegations are controversial and notoriously difficult to prove or disprove, partly because they concern imponderable factors rather than hard facts, and partly because they reflect the values and priorities of interest groups.

Nevertheless, the current unprecedented criticism of the performance of schools is seen by many countries as an opportunity to re-examine aims and practices and to reorder priorities with a view to seeking all-round improvement. The discussion below is organised under a number of key problems around which the current policy debate revolves.

THE LOW ACHIEVEMENT PROBLEM

Among the numerous problems facing schools, one is paramount: how better to serve the needs of the large group of pupils which gains little benefit from long years spent in the classroom. All countries recognise the phenomenon of the low achiever, the pupil who makes an effort but has difficulty in mastering the basic skills of reading, writing, counting, and communicating, or the pupil who is simply not motivated to learn. The great majority of countries are concerned that a high percentage of school leavers do not have suitable qualifications to present to employers and some countries now register that a significant percentage of school leavers is functionally illiterate. Too many children quit compulsory schooling with no sense of achievement or with only slight success.

In the past, this was not necessarily seen as a tragedy on the grounds that not all children could succeed and, indeed, some people believed that the social system required "failures" to perform unskilled tasks – that is, young adults who did not feel entitled, by their educational achievement, to the more rewarding and lucrative jobs. Moreover, in times of full employment, failure in school was not usually viewed as failure in life by the less successful individual, for he or she could still establish a place in society. In recent years, however, that passive response to school failure has become untenable as our conception of both human and working conditions has changed. This has led to a search for ways not only to understand failures but also to devise a range of strategies that will compensate for its causes, alleviate and ultimately overcome it – even if by means beyond the formal traditional school.

A major reason why greater prominence is given to the problem of low achievement today is the simple fact that young people remain in a school setting for a very long time. The age for starting one form or another of pre-primary schooling keeps falling and a steadily increasing percentage of young people stay on after the compulsory school to complete all, or the greater part of, the upper secondary cycle. This extension of the period of schooling has been accompanied in most OECD countries by the deferment of academic selection[2] and the retention of mixed-ability grouping throughout the primary cycle and, depending on the country, for part or the whole of the lower secondary cycle. The consequence is that, on the one hand, teachers must try to cope with a wide band of ability and, on the other hand, a large number of pupils struggle to keep up with a curriculum designed originally for a minority of high-achieving pupils who had been academically streamed. This underscores the importance currently attached to curriculum changes in many countries as a main objective of educational reform. In this situation, many low-achievers become first frustrated and then eventually cease trying. Their disaffection is usually further compounded by the anxieties of early maturity which can lead them into open or tacit conflict with the expectations and values of their teachers. Their years spent in school become progressively unfruitful and they get increasingly alienated.

A second factor has emerged since the mid-seventies to make the plight of low-achievers more serious; that is the sharp contraction of job opportunities for the young. At least, in the past, those who disliked school could stoically count the days before taking up a job, gaining adult status, and having money to spend of their own. Now they despair of the future as much as of the present because they know, or at least fear, that there will be no job to go to when the time comes to leave school. Their chances of finding work will be all the less in that they will not be able to present potential employers with a credible qualification. Failure in school foreshadows failure in the labour market.

Society is far from indifferent to their bleak prospects. On the contrary, what is to be done about the young unemployed has become a major public priority and a constant preoccupation of the news-media. Indeed, that preoccupation largely accounts for the unwonted limelight today being cast upon the schools. For, despite the evidence that high youth unemployment is primarily a consequence of economic recession combined with structural changes in the labour market, there are suddenly numerous critics to proclaim that the schools are mainly to blame because they turn out under-educated young people. This sort of criticism carries more weight than its faulty reasoning merits[3] because it coincides with rising public expectations of education in general, increasingly canalised into a demand for more quality and more open accountability of educational institutions to the community. While not necessarily accepting the view that there has been a qualitative decline in educational provision, many countries are beginning to recognise that the basic skills provided by schools are not in line with the needs of adult life in societies and economies experiencing rapid technological change and that they are, manifestly, not high enough for those who leave school unqualified. Schools must be attuned, therefore, to the necessity of continually raising their standards and regularly updating the knowledge and skills regarded as basic to their pupils' future lives.

The question, then, is how are schools to be made more effective? There is general agreement on what their aims ought to be: to help each pupil fulfil his or her potential; to raise overall national levels of educational attainment; to bring about greater equality of educational opportunity, if not outcomes; to foster social and cultural cohesion. Such aims are easy to state but difficult to pursue in that they entail instituting fundamental reforms in systems that have become resistant to, or suspicious of, change. Post-war reforms have often been mainly structural, affecting the ways that pupils are brought together for schooling but having little effect on institutional values and practices. Within the social context of the school, pupils' options and opportunities have continued to be restricted by the typical organisational features of age, grade, streaming, external assessment and teaching of discrete subjects. School reforms cannot be effective until their frame of reference is altered to one that engages pupils, teachers, administrators and families together in determining the services that schools offer. Positive and operational guidelines are required in order to translate aims into practice – the cardinal aim of enabling every young person to obtain personal satisfaction from being in school, finish up with adequate knowledge and skills and, above all, develop the capacity to continue to learn. These measures must apply to the ways schools are organised, to the curriculum and its assessment, and to the tasks of teachers – issues which are discussed below and in which the problem of low achievement remains a dominant concern.

DIMENSIONS FOR REFORM

Organisational Issues

Most of the major organisational reforms in, and experiments with, compulsory schooling in recent years have been made precisely in an attempt to assist pupils who, because of their social background, environment, sex or race, find difficulty in becoming integrated into schools and the broad stream of society and in sharing learning opportunities on equal terms. These have included: common schooling, mixed-ability teaching, new examination arrangements and special programmes such as 'head start' and 'educational priority areas'[4].

The spread of the common school has been, arguably, the most remarkable feature of educational changes in many OECD countries during the past twenty years or so. Though mainly impelled by an egalitarian philosophy, it has also been encouraged on pedagogical grounds and for reasons of cost and administrative tidiness. Parallel forms of school, with early selection to academic secondary education, have steadily been replaced by a system of stages within the range of primary and lower secondary education. Indeed, in a few countries, the common school has become coterminous with compulsory schooling. Children start at the age of six or seven and stay in the same school until they are fifteen. In the majority of countries, however, children spend four or five years in a primary school and then four or five years in lower secondary education or the middle school. In yet other countries, the nine to ten years are divided into three approximately equal sections. These variations often stem from political or administrative decisions made long ago and do not reflect empirical findings about the personality stages of child development.

As a rule, the primary school is non-selective, serving all the children in its immediate vicinity. Structural differentiation begins at the lower secondary level. A few countries retain a nationwide system of parallel secondary schools, based on selection. Several countries maintain parallel schools in some districts and common schools in others. The majority of countries, however, has abandoned selection at the end of the primary school and established the common or comprehensive lower secondary school. It might be inferred that a sharp polarisation exists between countries that have opted to retain selection and those that have opted for the common school. In fact, the crux is how much differentiation occurs within individual schools and when it begins. In practice, common schools vary considerably in the way they distribute pupils in classes and groups and apply the curriculum. The failure and low-achievement problem remains largely unsolved regardless of the school model that has been adopted. This phenomenon is not easy to document in precise numbers, but its dimensions can be illustrated by data available for four countries with different school models. In France, in 1980, 12 per cent of a cohort were early drop-outs from lower secondary vocational education, while 17 per cent of the same cohort did not go beyond lower secondary education. In Italy, in 1981, 18 per cent of the cohort did not obtain the *"licenza media"* while 16 per cent did not continue to any type of formal post-compulsory education and training. The figures for Germany (1980) were 10 per cent leaving school before the tenth year with another 10 per cent not continuing beyond compulsory schooling. The latter figure for Sweden (1981) was 21 per cent, while 8 per cent of the cohort had to be given special courses at the lower secondary level[5].

It does not seem that enough has been done to capitalise on the longer time young people spend in school. When the primary school constituted the whole or the greater part of initial education for most pupils, it had terminal tasks to fulfil. Now that it occupies only a half to two-thirds of the period that all young people spend in school, its curriculum, methods and, above all, modes of assessment have been open to appropriate modification. For example, descriptive and verbal reporting can effectively replace norm-referenced assessment, as several countries have discovered. Above all, primary and secondary education could be better articulated.

At present, there is in most countries a marked transition from primary to lower secondary school that is fraught with problems for low-achievers. The transition is characterised by a change from class teachers to subject specialist teachers and from a smaller, more socially intimate school unit to a larger one with a distinctly different ethos. Several countries have taken steps to ease the transition. A simple measure is to supply the receiving school with full information about each pupil's strengths and weaknesses. In many countries, attempts are made to augment such information by means of personal contacts and by taking primary pupils on visits to their future secondary school. Some education authorities have created a middle school designed to serve as a bridging institution between primary and secondary schooling, maintaining the class teacher system for most purposes but using specialists as well. Others try to reduce the effect of switching from class teacher to subject teacher by expecting each teacher to offer two or three subjects in the earlier secondary classes. Reduced division of labour among teachers is also used to increase pupil and teacher contacts in countries where secondary school teaching is not too specialised. Teachers may also cooperate in teams to deal with a large cohort of pupils, a pattern actively promoted in the Scandinavian countries.

In addition, there is a trend in some education systems to arrange for pupils to have the same class teacher for a number of successive years. This necessitates abandonment of the traditional practice of each teacher in the primary school being confined more or less permanently to dealing every year with children of the same age, for example seven-year-olds. During the primary school it is not too difficult to choose between two options:

  a) for the same teacher to take an age cohort right through the whole cycle;
  b) for one teacher to take an age cohort through the first three years and for another teacher to take them through the next two or three years.

In lower secondary education, that is, from the sixth or seventh to the ninth or tenth year, problems increasingly arise in an age group having the same class teacher continuously, but the practice is feasible and of great benefit to all pupils, regardless of their abilities.

The disjunction between primary and secondary school can be eliminated, or at least greatly diminished, if the entire range of compulsory schooling is designed as a unitary system. The Danish basic school affords, within the OECD family, one example of how to promote optimal continuity of class groups and sustained personal contact between a class teacher and pupils. Whenever possible, schools cater for the full range of compulsory schooling as well as pre-school year and a voluntary additional year for 16 to 17-year-olds. A teacher formally qualified to teach the mother tongue and one other subject at all levels will often be responsible for the same group of pupils throughout their nine years of compulsory schooling. Recent changes in Norwegian teacher education and proposals currently under consideration in Sweden also indicate a move towards a modified class-teacher system in the lower secondary stages. Swedish practice introduces specialisation by stages and facilitates continuity by training teachers to operate on several levels.

In this context, reference is appropriate to the actual and potential value of *alternative schools*. Broadly conceived, alternative schools have always existed where there has been a tradition of private as well as public education. Today, there is a trend in some countries to set up alternative schools within the public sector. The idea of an "alternative" school is attractive to some parents and teachers when they find the ordinary schools too set in their curricula and methods or not sufficiently motivating, or, in some instances, intellectually demanding of their pupils. In other cases, such schools are designed to meet the special needs of children who are in difficulty in conventional education. Groups of parents, in close collaboration with like-minded teachers, then seek to run schools according to their own principles. In the United States, the metaphor of "magnet" schools has become fashionable with its suggestion that children are fully motivated when the school ethos and curriculum reflect their special interests. Alternative schools might certainly seem to fit in with contemporary notions about democratic participation in school management and parental power.

There is, however, an equity issue lying behind the enthusiasm among certain parents and education authorities in some countries for alternative schools. A majority of parents really have no liberty in the choice of a school for their children. For them, it is the nearest school or nothing. Where there is complete liberty of choice, the sophisticated and well-to-do usually secure places for their children in the schools known to achieve the best academic results. True freedom of choice also presupposes that parents are all equally well informed about the special characteristics and performances of the schools within their communities. There is also the risk that, as some alternative schools attract bright and privileged pupils, others will come to be used as isolation centres for delinquent and slow-achieving pupils. This is not to argue that support for alternative schools is misconceived but simply to point out that they may operate to the detriment of the general aims of schooling if suitable precautions are not taken. In the best conditions, alternative schools can bring new ideas and processes into general educational practice.

An important aspect of school organisation is the extent of differentiation which exists within schools. A variety of attitudes towards *internal differentiation* is to be found among OECD countries. The prevailing view in the United States is that those in need of remedial or accelerated education should be regularly identified by standardised achievement tests and that courses and textbooks should be designed to suit the ability level of the pupil. In the United Kingdom, more differentiation is desired within the curriculum to suit the variations in abilities and aptitudes of pupils; specifically, mathematics and science courses should be designed for differing levels of ability and not for all students. Japan sees a need at the primary level for supplementary instruction for slow learners, individualised teaching and ability-group teaching. In Norway, however, age groups are now kept together till the end of compulsory school. Finland proposes to retain the unified comprehensive school and, indeed, is removing ability groups in foreign languages and mathematics in the upper grades of the lower secondary school.

Similar variations exist in Member countries with regard to *attendance patterns.* The prevailing patterns of the distribution and length of the school day, week and year, the length of lessons and the time to be devoted to homework were introduced long ago to fit in with the social and industrial conditions then prevailing but are not necessarily compatible with the conditions of today nor with the contemporary objectives of compulsory schooling. Some examples will illustrate the variations from one country to another. The number of days of annual attendance ranges from 175 in France up to 240 in Germany and Spain. The number of hours of weekly attendance ranges from 18 in the first year of school in Denmark up to 35 from the fifth year onwards in Sweden. Whereas in some countries (for example, Spain, France and the Netherlands) the duration of the school week is the same irrespective of the age of pupils, in others (for example, Denmark) it varies according to the pupils' ages – the younger the pupils the shorter the week. Again the length of classes varies from 45 minutes to 60 minutes between countries.

There has been relatively little investigation of the effects of different attendance patterns in terms of children's learning rhythms, powers of concentration, physical health and emotional satisfaction as well as in the light of what is best for teachers, parents and the community. What are the merits of a four-term as opposed to a three-term year? Should the traditional long summer holiday be reduced and the period saved be used to provide longer winter and spring holidays? Disadvantaged children often lose ground during the long summer recess. What is the ideal length of the school day? Is it better to start early in the morning and finish in the early afternoon or to start and finish the day later? How long should class periods be? Or should the very notion of periods be abandoned? With a view to realising a freer and more enjoyable school life without lowering educational standards, Japan has reduced the standard school hours for each subject area, and school hours have been allowed to be adjusted in a creative and ingenious way in conformity with actual conditions in each region and school. France has recently opted for periods with an average length of 45 minutes. In all cases, the key question is whether there exists a positive link between the number of hours pupils devote to study both in school and at home and the standards achieved. If such a link does exist, then it follows that prevailing attendance patterns require revision.

The Curriculum

Much of the current criticism of schools is levelled specifically at the curriculum. Many argue that the content is too diffused and too abstract to provide a useful training for life, that there are too many options and too much individual choice and that teaching methods are too permissive. As a consequence, it is further argued, pupils are not motivated to work hard and to sufficient purpose so that it is not surprising if many of them leave school to all intents and purposes illiterate, innumerate and with lazy minds.

The spectrum covered by the curriculum during compulsory schooling has indeed expanded considerably in all countries during recent years. There has also been a movement towards pupil-centred or individualised learning, although it is not clear how much teachers really support it. Moreover, the shift in emphasis from a purely cognitive diet to all-round intellectual and social development has required schools to assume a far wider responsibility for the learning experiences of their pupils. Many schools have strengthened their socialisation function, organised voluntary leisure activities, encouraged discussion in the later years of sexual matters, racial issues, war and peace, drug problems, popular culture and the mass media, and have allocated increasingly more time and resources to preparing pupils for working life.

Critics of the wider curriculum claim, however, that the move from "didactic teaching" to "socialisation" and the adoption of permissive teaching methods inspired by pupil-centred curriculum theory have in practice undermined the pupil's mastery of basic cognitive skills, especially numeracy and literacy, and led to a general decline in academic standards. There is not, however, always a clear idea of what concentration on basic knowledge and skills should constitute, beyond insistence upon reading, writing, numeracy and, sometimes, oral communication.

The "back to basics" demand is now being merged in many countries into the idea of a *core curriculum*, advocated by both traditionalists, on pedagogical grounds, and by reformists, on equity grounds. It is felt that in recent years too much time has been devoted to feeding pupils with a mass of "desirable" knowledge rather than to ensuring that they command fully a range of "necessary" knowledge. If the content of the school curriculum is reduced, then more problem-centred methods may be used and pupils may develop their conceptual and creative abilities, with a stress on learning how to learn, the manipulation of ideas and intellectual discovery. The time allowed for mastering skills or frames of knowledge should be treated as a variable and unlocked from age grades, with all pupils studying a broad range of subjects up to a maximum level, even at the expense of optional subjects.

Core curricula vary only slightly from country to country. The following subjects consistently emerge: communications and language skills; numeracy and mathematics; science and technology; social and environmental understanding; vocational studies; physical and mental recreational activities; creative arts; interpersonal skills. There has also recently been great stress in a number of countries on the particular importance of mathematics, science and technology.

Where the evidence is unequivocal that a significant or large percentage of pupils is under-achieving, it is realistic to recognise that all needs cannot be equally satisfied and that curriculum priorities may have to be established. The first priority might then be to ensure that every pupil shall be helped to attain an agreed level of competence in the basic skills, even if this implies devoting more resources to some pupils than to others – for example, by maintaining lower teacher/pupil ratios in remedial classes for low achievers. The second could be to offer all children a common curriculum consisting of the topics listed above, at least until the year (in principle, the year before the end of compulsory schooling) when it becomes clear who will stay on at school and who will depart at the statutory leaving age. Alongside the core curriculum, a range of optional subjects would be offered in timetables. A third priority would be to set aside periods in the timetable specifically designed to help those who plan to leave school at the end of the compulsory period or soon after.

There is virtually complete agreement among OECD countries that education for working life, as provided within compulsory schooling, should not aim at preparation for specific occupations, but should be treated as part of general education and include teaching and guidance about working life and training requirements in different occupations, the way the labour market operates, collective bargaining, and the role of major industries in the national economy. Ironically, "employable skills", the ones commonly mentioned by those who argue that schools should prepare pupils better for working life, accord well with what schools seek to develop anyway: literacy, an ability to communicate orally, numeracy, manual dexterity, an ability to cooperate with others, habits of hard work, not to speak of learning to learn. Independent critical thinking is also likely to make young persons valuable and productive, though occasionally troublesome, in places of employment[6].

A strong practical element in the curriculum undoubtedly makes daily life in school more attractive to many young people and helps to hold the attention of the low achiever, but it can be costly. Art and music, experimental sciences, experience with wood, metal and electronics, typing, gymnastics and games are all expensive to provide. For this reason, some schools share expensive facilities and some education authorities have established centres where pupils can use practical facilities both during and outside normal school hours.

The process by which changes to curricula are identified and implemented is a very complex one which has been described in earlier OECD reports[7]. Such changes emanate from external political and social pressures, the innovatory enthusiasm of principals, individual teachers and groups of teachers and, not infrequently, the wishes of older pupils. It is extremely difficult for schools to build and sustain a curriculum that consistently meets with general satisfaction. The recent accent in some countries on school-based curriculum reform[8] reflects the central role that schools themselves have to play but it also underlines the conflict that such individual school initiatives might create vis-a-vis nationally set objectives and criteria. This, in turn, has led many countries to recognise the need for establishing new national mechanisms, or reinforcing existing ones, to ensure that the curriculum is constantly monitored and revised in the light of changing conditions and expectations.

A main problem which confronts efforts to reform the curriculum is the traditional emphasis that school systems place on *examination and accreditation*. Examinations remain in most OECD countries an inescapable component of the curriculum. They are meant to ensure that the young are prepared and accredited for adult roles in society and constitute a powerful control mechanism. They can lead ineluctably to continuing social stratification by penalising those who are slow to command verbal skills. On the other hand, it can be argued that accreditation is a prerequisite for a shift from ascription, that is unjust, to achievement as the means of allocating roles in society.

It is obviously essential that in one way or another the progress of each pupil through the school should be monitored so that learning deficiencies and problems can be diagnosed as early as possible in the primary school and that suitable guidance can be given about the choice of subjects, especially at the lower secondary level. It is equally important that a young person should leave school with some kind of profile report indicating his or her learning achievements, or at least experience, and his personal qualities, if only as something to show a would-be employer. Such a report should give useful information about school leavers and, while safeguarding them against discrimination, it would protect employers from taking on inadequately qualified employees. One measure to be considered is that of systematically applying diagnostic and aptitude tests at critical stages, notably at the transition from primary to secondary school and, say, at the age of thirteen.

All this points to the desirability of ensuring that criterion-referenced assessment should complement norm-referenced assessment, though this is by no means easy to devise. But increasingly, examinations are being made available to most children rather than a few. The middle school certificate, such as *Mittlere Reife* in Germany, the *Brevet d'études du premier cycle* (BEPC) in France and the Certificate of Elementary Education in Spain, all tend to be attainable at various levels by the majority of pupils (often as much as 80 per cent of the population and 100 per cent in the case of Sweden). Unquestionably, developments in guidance, testing and reporting have ensured that the diagnoses of the schools have had increasing importance in determining access to different occupational and social roles. These developments are occurring in most systems.

Education authorities at all levels require hard data about pupil achievement in order to monitor trends and to respond to allegations of falling standards. Some countries are resorting to national or state wide testing programmes, e.g. the Assessment Performance Unit in the United Kingdom and the NAEP (National Assessment of Educational Progress) in the United States, based on light sampling of pupils and aimed at producing achievement profiles over different areas of the curriculum for the whole country or broad sub-categories (e.g. boys versus girls, rural versus urban schools). They are also intended to permit comparison of levels of achievement over time. With the aid of matrix sampling, they can cover a broad range of competences and sub-skills. Such programmes focus on checking folklore evidence on the effectiveness of compulsory schooling and on pinpointing areas of schooling where improvement or additional support is needed. Other programmes focus on a smaller number of tests (usually in basic skills) and are applied to the whole age group. They aim at smaller geographical or institutional units and primarily serve to complement less standardised forms of pupil examination and to focus educational activities on key goals. The utility and methodological adequacy of large-scale testing is highly controversial and raises several issues. The fact, however, remains that education authorities need to have a basis for determining whether the achievement of individuals and schools matches the needs of the day and whether it is as high as possible given the resources available.

Teachers and Their Tasks

One vital prerequisite for effective schooling for low as well as high achievers is to employ teachers who are professionally well qualified and fully motivated. Yet the contribution of teachers to educational reforms has all too often been overlooked or underestimated in plans for implementation. The great majority of them are not given any special orientation in order to prepare for new roles. The result is that reforms come and go but many teachers continue using the same methods and generally behaving exactly as before. Many resist the very idea of change. So, narrow subject specialisation remains common, pupils remain streamed and academic values dominant as does the pursuit of good examination results for the gifted, though the latter would no longer be a preoccupation if examinations were to be abolished.

In most countries, the authorities have recently reduced the size of their teaching forces or slowed down their past rate of increase, very largely by restricting the annual intake to teacher training institutions, either by reducing enrolments or simply by closing some down. Scaling down the number of teachers in schools gives rise to acute staffing problems, particularly in those countries where primary school teachers are still trained in one type of establishment, secondary school teachers in another and pre-school teachers in a third. To overcome this diversity, some countries are reflecting on the case for establishing an all-graduate teaching profession, or at least the experience of a common training trunk for all teachers. Such reforms are not without their difficulties, particularly because secondary school teachers remain essentially subject-based. But they would be particularly desirable on practical grounds at a time when enrolments in primary schooling in most countries are falling sharply and the demand for teachers is falling correspondingly. Teachers are all the more likely to lose their jobs if they are neither permitted nor sufficiently qualified to teach in secondary schools. If all teachers were to have a similar basic training then mobility within the entire compulsory cycle would be facilitated[9].

The morale of teachers is being undermined not only by the contraction of their profession but also by pressures to change their teaching styles and methods, to broaden their social experience and to yield much or at least some of their classroom autonomy. How can those in initial training be best prepared to cope with these pressures and how can established teachers be helped to adapt to them? Modifications are evidently required in the organisation, style and content of initial training. There is also great scope for professional adaptation and renewal through expanded and updated in-service training, both in special institutions and at the level of each school[10].

As things are, teacher training in most countries is still overwhelmingly confined to pre-service preparation. At the same time, most national education authorities now recognise that there is a strong case for modifying the present balance between pre-service training and continuing training on-the-job. This is not to imply that teachers should be expected to embrace all the latest ideas, theories and methods. It does imply, however, that they should be expected to take part in ad hoc programmes at district and regional level together with school-based professional development activities, all designed to keep them up-to-date as well as informed of the aims of educational reforms and their implications both for the curriculum and pedagogical practice. In other words, continuing training should be an integral part of the teachers' professional life and related to each teacher's perceived interests and needs. For both initial and continuing training, a major need will be to build up an innovative and flexible corps of teacher trainers.

Diversifying school services by vesting more authority within the school community does not of itself demand additional teaching resources; but it does make it difficult for schools with insufficient staff to respond sensitively to their pupils. The variable of teacher time appears to be crucial to school improvement. In order to take the lead in their schools in processes that engage parents or result in changes to organisational structures, curriculum content or pedagogical methods, teachers require time to glean ideas, disseminate information and to reflect upon and synthesise experiences other than their own.

CONCLUDING REMARKS: THE QUALITY OF SCHOOLING

As argued in the OECD Report on Compulsory Schooling, qualitative factors distinguish, in the last analysis, the performance of one school from that of another. Recent research findings have shown that the same material inputs to what appear to be similar schools, in terms of the socio-economic background of the pupils and other key characteristics, often produce very dissimilar results[11]. At the same time, politicians and educational administrators have become wary of throwing more money at schools without some attempt to match outputs to inputs. They speculate whether there is not a ceiling beyond which quantitative inputs to schools have no effect or an effect incommensurate with the extra increase in expenditure. Education authorities are accordingly under strong pressure to bring about qualitative improvements in the schools.

Specific efforts are under way throughout OECD countries to improve the performance of the less successful schools and to raise overall standards of achievement. Although by no means in agreement that standards have fallen over the last decade or so, all these countries concur that every young person is entitled to the best education that society can provide and that this necessitates constant vigilance to ensure that the curriculum is responsive to new demands upon it and that high standards are consistently maintained.

A joint United States/OECD international conference[12] identified the main factors that education authorities must bear in mind in formulating policy. These may be summarised as follows:

i) to clarify and where necessary redefine national goals for compulsory schooling. This might entail studying successful goal models and indicators both within and across countries with a view to developing systematic procedures for translating goals into practice;

ii) to enable all pupils to acquire a set of basic learning skills through the adoption of a core curriculum characterised by balance, breadth, relevance and appropriate differentiation;

iii) to ensure that the goals of the school are accurately reflected in its organisation;

iv) to ensure that there is a good match between teacher qualifications and teacher tasks, that there is within each school a range of teaching skills to deal with all learner needs and abilities, and that there is competent management and deployment of all the available teaching resources;

v) to provide effective school leadership through close collaboration between pupils, teachers, principals, parents and members of the community;

vi) to develop effective ways and means of assessing educational progress within schools and at community, regional and national levels.

All those concerned – policy-makers, administrators, educational researchers, principals and teachers – are well aware that it is easy to state such aims but extremely difficult in practice to implement them because too little is known about the interaction of the factors that would conduce to success. Systematic and long-term research into the dynamics of effective schooling is therefore called for.

NOTES AND REFERENCES

1. For the whole of this chapter, see *Compulsory Schooling in a Changing World,* OECD, Paris, 1983.

2. *Selection and Certification in Education and Employment,* OECD, Paris, 1977.

3. See "The Role of Education and Training in Relation to the Employment and Unemployment of Young People", Statement by the Education Committee, OECD, Paris, 1983, (document for general distribution).

4. For a detailed analysis, see *Compulsory Schooling in a Changing World, op. cit.*

5. *Education and Training after Basic Schooling,* OECD, Paris, 1985.

6. See "The Competences Needed in Working Life", OECD, Paris, 1982 (document for general distribution).

7. See, in particular, *Handbook on Curriculum Development,* OECD/CERI, Paris, 1975.

8. *School-based Curriculum Development,* OECD/CERI, Paris, 1979.

9. See *Teacher Policies in a New Context,* OECD, Paris, 1979.

10. *In-Service Education and Training of Teachers: A Condition for Educational Change*, OECD/CERI, Paris, 1982.

11. M. Rutter *et al.*, *Fifteen Thousand Hours: Secondary Schools and Their Effects on Children*, Open Books, London, 1979.

12. International Conference on Quality in Education held in Washington D.C., 1st-3rd May 1984.

74

Chapter 7

THE NEW POST-COMPULSORY SECTOR OF EDUCATION AND TRAINING[1]

THE CHALLENGES FACING POST-COMPULSORY EDUCATION AND TRAINING

Education and training for 16-19 year-olds are central to current policy concerns, explicable by a number of main factors. Demand and enrolments at this level have increased significantly across OECD countries, particularly in vocational education and in a range of "non-formal" training schemes, though in general education too in some countries. Youth unemployment levels are very high and still growing. More young people are now unemployed for spells of longer duration rather than for short periods, and the employment situation of young adults aged 20-24 has deteriorated over recent years. The demographic fact of increased numbers of young people coming from secondary schools looking for jobs or further education and training has exacerbated this already very difficult situation. Together these factors mean that transition to adulthood – once the relatively rapid transfer from school to work for all but the minority continuing in further and higher education – is now a lengthy, drawn-out and uncertain process for a large proportion of young people after their completion of initial education.

This process of transition is, nonetheless, lived by groups and individuals in quite different ways; the experience of the unqualified school leaver with minimal short-term job prospects remains a world apart from the academic high achiever destined for an extended stay in higher education. Yet the changing nature of adolescence raises a number of conflicts that are felt generally, even if in different ways. These have been described as follows:

"Young people are today caught in a squeeze between many conflicting forces. They mature biologically one to two years earlier than did their counterparts some fifty years ago but they stay longer in school and assume important adult responsibilities much later. There is also a lack of consistency in how young people are treated: in some countries at the age of 18 they have the right to vote but not the right to participate in decision-making in their educational institutions. They want to establish adult identity as holders of occupations but are not wanted at the work places. They do not want to stay in a school with all the pressures for achievements and irrelevance of curriculum, but are fully aware that the number of educational credentials they can amass determines their subsequent careers".[2]

These changes and conflicts illuminate the challenges facing the post-compulsory sector – in the past, not really constituting a distinct sector at all – and help explain why it has come to occupy a place of special prominence. How to offer diverse learning opportunities that meet the interests of a broad cross-section of young people in the latter years of their teens? How to provide education and training that will be useful in such a difficult job market? How to establish reasonable alternatives to unemployment, and how to avoid the most glaring social injustices that the sorting and selection at this stage can give rise to? These questions have led countries to look increasingly at the availability and distribution of education and training opportunities for young people in their teens and early twenties as a whole. However interpreted by different Member countries, there is a growing *public responsibility* for young people. In some countries, this means the right to upper secondary education. The extent of public responsibility has been taken further in others in the form of a youth guarantee[3], which grants rights to education but also entails an obligation on the part of public authorities to ensure a place in education, training or work for all young people up to a certain age (mainly 18 years). Transition to adulthood in the 1980s, therefore, cannot only be typified as a more drawn-out and uncertain process than in the past. It also takes place increasingly under the charge of public authorities, but with the active participation of industry in providing training opportunities and work experience.

Education and training issues can thus be seen in the broader context of overall youth policies[4] and this focuses attention on the needs and interests of all young people instead of considering in relative isolation the various institutions or sectors where young people are found. But the fact remains that the post-compulsory sector is also very diverse and now contains students and trainees of quite differing expectations, abilities, and future prospects. Even in those countries that have a highly uniform structure of provision for the 16-19 year-old group, the needs and aims of the students vary widely and strategies to deal with them must face the perennial tension between the transfer (to higher education) and terminal functions of education and training at this level. Despite the fact that there is a gamut of institutional differences among countries, the main patterns of provision in Member countries can be categorised into three broad approaches or models each deriving from the traditions and priorities obtaining in each country.

MAIN PATTERNS OF PROVISION[5]

These approaches or models of provision can be identified as the "schooling" model, the "dual" model, and the "mixed" model. These are described below in turn.

The "Schooling" Model

The main characteristic of the "schooling" model is that it aims at integrating most, if not all, forms of provision after compulsory schooling within the formal education system, favouring schooling on a full-time basis for the majority of the age group. This pattern characterises the countries that pioneered mass full secondary education, the United States and Canada, which now have 87 per cent and 72 per cent respectively of 17 year-olds enrolled in the formal education system[6]. At present, it finds its fullest expression in Japan where 94 per cent of the relevant age group attend upper-secondary schools. In many European countries the formal school system dominates provision at this level. In Belgium and Sweden it has a virtual monopoly, and the school sector is prominent in the Netherlands, Finland, Denmark, and, to a somewhat lesser degree, France. In all of these, schools currently enrol more than two-thirds of the 17 year-old age group and there have recently been policy statements issued favouring a still further coverage of the school system especially for 16 and 17 year-olds.

Within this overall pattern of provision is a variety of policies and practices. The presence of an older student body in upper secondary systems of Western Europe, together with the higher proportion of the age group in technical-vocational branches, gives a pattern of provision that is considerably different from that in the United States, Japan and certain of the Canadian provinces. This is illustrated by the fact that a significant proportion of 18 and 19 year-olds attend Community Colleges in the United States and Junior Colleges in Japan, that are part of their further and higher education systems, following courses which offer a wide range of general and technical programmes whose contents are sometimes similiar to those of European upper secondary schools. It should be noted that in several countries with significantly lower levels of enrolment in post-compulsory provision – for instance, Turkey, Portugal, Spain and Greece – schools are also dominant.

The "Dual" Model

The distinguishing characteristic of this approach is a strong and highly developed apprenticeship sector as found in the German-speaking OECD countries – Germany, Switzerland and Austria. This developed form of vocational preparation is termed "dual" because it combines training within firms with part-time schooling, but the overall model can also be described as "dual" since within their formal education and training systems there coexist the general, academic institutions and the apprenticeship sector. These three German-speaking countries are the only examples among the OECD countries where the proportion enrolled in apprenticeships is higher than that for students attending school on a full-time basis. Since they have compulsory part-time education up to the age of 18, their overall participation rates for the 16 to 19 year age group are among the highest of all OECD countries. It should be noted that there are other countries that have a smaller, though still significant, apprenticeship sector – though one that is predominantly male. Australia, Denmark, France, Italy, the Netherlands and Norway are good examples. Caution is required, however, in making comparisons of overall figures since the scope, duration and status of apprenticeship training varies considerably within as well as among Member countries.

It is a feature, then, of the dual systems that full-time upper secondary schools recruit a relatively low proportion of the age group which have few links with the large apprenticeship sector. There are signs, however, of greater emphasis upon schooling in these countries and of a narrowing gap between the schooling and dual approaches to education and training. Indications of this are the generalisation of an additional year of full-time education beyond compulsory schooling in some regions of Germany, Switzerland and Austria, the recent development of full-time vocational schools (Berufsfachschulen – now catering for some 10 per cent of the age group in Germany) and the rapid increase in enrolments in general education in Germany. It should be emphasized that this has not necessarily been at the expense of vocational or dual forms of education and, in no small part, reflects the trend to postpone entry to an apprenticeship with the completion of a longer general education.

The "Mixed" Model

The "mixed" approach is characterised by the greater importance assigned to training in the non-formal sector. It is typically found where schools represent the current dominant form of provision and where the overall potential for growth at the post-compulsory level is still relatively high. Behind its development is the viewpoint that the formal system, and schools in particular, cannot or should not monopolise expansion. Thus, while some expansion of the established school and apprenticeship systems is not inconsistent with a "mixed" approach, it essentially supports development of separate initial training schemes outside schools and distinct from more formal programmes, with an active role for industry in providing opportunities.

At present, the best example of the "mixed" approach is the United Kingdom where a special agency, the Manpower Services Commission under the Ministry of Employment, has the responsibility and resources to organise training for about 40 per cent of the age group not catered for by the formal education and training system[7]. Schools, colleges and education administrations, however, can and do participate in these schemes mostly as partners for services provided on a contractual basis.

Presenting these as "models" should not detract from the extent of overlap in the pressures felt and developments current in each country, nor should it suggest that they are fixed and immutable. Certain changes of emphasis within the "dual" approach have already been mentioned. A further example of this, though one that is more controversial, is the gradual introduction in German schools of a full-time vocational year following initial education with the aim that it be recognised as the first year of certain apprenticeships and there are also signs of an increased formalisation of the training within enterprises.

One evident constraint upon countries that wish to incorporate larger elements of within-enterprise training as part of their 16-19 provision is the scarcity of places for trainees, which in turn reflects the very difficult labour market faced by this age group. It is as yet unclear, for example, how this will affect the implementation of proposals now being seriously discussed in some countries (as in Sweden and Yugoslavia) to introduce obligatory periods of work experience into academic lines of study.

It is also unclear how far the "mixed" approach, as exemplified in the United Kingdom, will remain distinct from the "dual" model with the passage of time. The major difference from the latter at present stems from the fact that the training is less formalised, being more recent and experimental. Yet, given that many of these training schemes incorporate the elements of both training provided in enterprises and the complementary learning based in colleges, they could come more closely to resemble the "dual" systems if these schemes become more permanent and established.

Countries categorised as following the "schooling" approach cover a wide range of institutional arrangements and are subject, equally, to change. Such is the importance assigned to the formal school and college system in many countries that specific consideration is given below to developments in upper secondary education.

DEVELOPMENTS IN UPPER SECONDARY EDUCATION

Many features of the present organisation of upper secondary schools can be seen as the result of marginal adjustments brought about by the need to expand provision as well as the outcome of coherent, active policies. Formal upper secondary institutions could also be characterised as particularly responsive to pressures and requirements stemming from the lower and higher layers of the education system between which they lie, to a certain neglect of goals and objectives germane to this level of schooling *per se*. The traditions out of which they grew reflect the influence exerted by compulsory schooling, on the one hand, and higher education on the other. In North America and Japan, upper secondary education developed as a direct extension of basic schooling and it adopted many of the features of "schools for children" in terms of similar teaching styles and the classroom setting, the maintainance of the "pupil" as well as the "teacher" status and the endowment of a relatively uniform educational and socialising experience for the majority of the age group.

Most European Member countries have followed a somewhat different line and the influence exerted by the higher level can be seen. In these countries, the dominant function of secondary education historically has been the selection and preparation of a social and intellectual minority for university studies. Instead of representing a continuation of basic schooling, there tended to be a sharp break between basic schooling and post-compulsory education and for traditional secondary programmes to be expanded without major reforms and changes. This led inevitably to a strong emphasis upon academic styles and values. It is in more recent years that the growth and diversity of upper secondary students has forced consideration of more far-reaching organisational and internal reforms.

One dominant organisational question concerns the appropriate form of institutions – should they be separate from, or integrated with, the lower secondary schools and what should be their links at the other end with the establishments of further and higher education? A fairly common pattern in OECD countries is the coexistence of full general secondary schools covering a wide age range (11/12 to 18/19 years) with post-16 vocational schools. In a number of countries with mass upper secondary school attendance (Japan, Sweden, Norway, Denmark, France, Italy), separate post-16 provision is the predominant mode. Arguments for and against institutional separation from the lower secondary school abound. Many fear the general consequences for secondary schools of removing two or three grades from the top. Support for their separation is given by the concern to reduce selection within lower secondary education and to give the upper secondary sector greater chance to develop its own distinctiveness and autonomy. It can be argued, in addition, that post-16 colleges offer a more favourable setting and climate for older adolescents. Establishing a more adult climate and appropriate pedagogical relations is especially important for the students who react against the atmosphere of the lower secondary school, many of whom, under happier employment conditions, would have looked to a job to give them adult status.

On the other hand, the social and psychological effects of isolating a narrowly-defined age group have also to be considered[8]. The narrowness of the age group in post-16 colleges can be widened to the degree that they also cater for older students; in other words, it depends on the rigidity of the boundaries between secondary and post-secondary education. Many examples exist of colleges that provide for students spanning this divide (e.g. Further Education Colleges in the United Kingdom, TAFE colleges in Australia, Lycées techniques in France), though in the majority of countries these arrangements are still on a rather small scale and predominantly in the technical/vocational sector. It is in the United States (with Community Colleges) and in some Canadian provinces (with, for example, the *Collèges d'enseignement général et professionnel*) that developments in the mainstream of formal education have led most notably to a greater mix of age groups and blurring of the boundary between secondary and post-secondary provision.

Faced by the need to reconsider policies for 16-19 year-olds, catering now for a more diverse student body, another major organisational question is the degree to which upper secondary institutions should be specialised or whether the different tracks and branches should be integrated. Until fairly recently, one of the guiding principles for the expansion of upper secondary institutions in the majority of Member countries, as with other areas and levels of education, was the closer integration of the options and programmes within larger, more comprehensive institutions. Equity considerations argued for greater homogeneity of schools and the establishment of larger, polyvalent institutions aiming to reduce hierarchical distinctions among the different programmes. As has been described above, however, countries have followed different paths of institutional development and are under increasing pressure to diversify their provision. The strains created by the pull of diversity, in the face of such a wide range of student's abilities, expectations and interests, are felt most acutely in those countries that went furthest towards integration at this level.

It is interesting to note that those European countries, such as Sweden and, to a lesser extent, Norway, that have an active policy to integrate more closely their general, technical and vocational education, do not interpret this as the introduction of a common core curriculum. Integration is primarily understood as the coexistence, within one or a small number of different institutions, of clearly-defined and structured lines of study, each leading to their own qualification; that is, integrated upper secondary schools serving all young people within a given catchment area are not viewed as incompatible with curriculum differentiation and specialisation. On the contrary, closer integration is seen as a strategy to give full upper secondary status to all options – in particular those in the vocational sector – since common provision is expected to attenuate hierarchical and status differences among programmes, to facilitate transfer between courses, and to bridge the gap between education and training.

In the United States and in Japan, where most students enrol in programmes of general academic education, lack of formal differentiation within schools has not prevented other kinds of informal, and very real, differentiation to emerge *among* schools, related in particular to the academic ability and the social background of students. The private sector, within the established school system or as complementary to it, has added to the degree of differentiation. The position of schools in the pecking order is basically determined, as elsewhere, by the chances they give to young people of entering the more selective establishments of higher education. At present, emphasis in the United States is upon greater uniformity of school programmes – one of the strongest criticisms currently voiced is that diversity is excessive with a very wide array of elective courses taken disparately by students – while in Japan, they are seeking to widen choice and diversity. The dilemmas and difficulties here are universal – how to strike a balance between giving a common education and socialisation experience to as many youngsters as possible while at the same time responding to the variety of needs and interests of students, the requirements of the labour market, and those of further and higher education?

The developments and the forms of differentiation discussed in this section have been presented in institutional and organisational terms. Yet the different styles and contents of the education and training provided in the various establishments, and the issue of specialisation versus integration, are essentially also curricular. These questions are examined more directly in the next section.

THE BRANCHES OF POST-COMPULSORY EDUCATION AND TRAINING

Large variations in the balance between general and technical/vocational education and training are found in OECD countries (recognising that these very distinctions are problematic in any discussion of curriculum.) A first group of countries can be distinguished, which includes most in Northern Continental Europe, where the technical/vocational sector is assigned particular importance and where between a half and two-thirds of the post-compulsory students are enrolled in these branches. These include Austria, France, Germany, Denmark, the Netherlands, Norway, Switzerland and Sweden. This can be contrasted with a second set of countries with high levels of overall enrolment and the "schooling" pattern of provision where the balance between the general and the technical/vocational is the reverse – two-thirds or more of students are in academic/general programmes. These include the North American countries and Japan. A number of others, with relatively low overall levels of post-compulsory participation and a dominant school sector, have a high proportion of the students in general education (e.g. the United Kingdom, Spain, Greece and Portugal). In these cases, more than half and up to 80 per cent of post-compulsory students are in general programmes.

In many places, recent policy has aimed to increase the scale of vocational education, both by channelling "new groups" of students into these branches and, in some cases, by altering the balance between general and technical/vocational studies. Attempts to reduce the share of general education have often not met with the success intended. In part, this is because of the difficulty of changing the preferences of students. But the fact that there has also been greater competition for entry into many vocational branches, with larger numbers of rejected candidates, indicates a mismatch between demand and supply and a gap between the intentions of policy and reality. The constraints on increasing the places in vocational education and training are several. The demographics of large teenage cohorts, the high costs involved in setting up vocational programmes, and the lack of traineeship places are major ones. Vocational education is often closely linked to the availability of workplace apprenticeship or training places and in the current economic situation it is more difficult to find sufficient openings in firms. This largely explains the falling participation rates in part-time vocational education in some countries (as in Australia and the United Kingdom) and the substantial number of drop-outs from these programmes in others, as in Scandinavian countries.

As students in post-compulsory education and training have grown in numbers and have become more diverse, this has led to greater differentiation within both the general and vocational branches. A major problem this raises in each case is how to prevent the courses and programmes perceived as "lower" sliding to the bottom of the pecking order and becoming residual options of last resort.

In *general/academic* education, differentiation in the form of a sharpened hierarchy among lines leading to the same qualification – different lines in the baccalauréat, Abitur or maturità for example – has been evident for some time (and discussed in more detail in Chapter 8 in relation to higher education). A more recent phenomenon is the growing difference emerging between general programmes geared primarily to entry to higher education and others with a more polyvalent orientation. As more young people continue in education and training after the minimum school leaving age, it is likely that the latter programmes, and particularly general studies with emphasis upon preparation for working life, will grow apace. The development of "higher preparatory courses" in Denmark, short, general studies in the Netherlands, "diploma" schools in Switzerland and pre-vocational courses elsewhere are examples, as are the shorter programmes within the same branches of longer-cycle upper secondary education, especially in social, commercial and humanistic studies (Sweden).

One of the main difficulties faced by these types of course, as mentioned above, is that they risk downgrading in the eyes of both students and potential employers. The low status of the non-college preparatory, general branch of senior high school in the United States shows that the risk is a real one. This deserves particular attention in the development of policies, especially as it is potentially an important area of provision. In recent years, growing recognition of the need to include subjects related to computer literacy and the use of new information technologies as part of general education have given added impetus to reflection and experimentation in this area. If they were successfully incorporated into, and recognised in, new general programmes, it would help establish an intermediary sector between the strictly academic and the vocational options and thus fill a vacuum that currently exists in many countries as a result of the clear, and largely anachronistic, dichotomy between education and training.

Sharpened differentiation in *vocational* education has occurred too. A "higher" level can often be distinguished from a "lower" one: the former including well-established programmes demanding strict standards of professional competence and a firm general basis, with the "lower" level leading to a basic qualification that is intended to facilitate transition to working life. Presenting vocational education as a dichotomy obviously oversimplifies the complex and varied situation that pertains in Member countries. But it is interesting that this dualism has been formalised in several countries. In France, the Netherlands, and Sweden, for example, there are two separate streams of vocational education. In Switzerland and Austria, full-time apprenticeships at a lower level than other apprenticeships have been formally introduced and there are other developments that indicate the trend towards greater differentiation within vocational education.

BRIDGING THE GAP BETWEEN EDUCATION AND TRAINING

In recent years, much of the expansion in vocational education has concentrated on the lower levels. With rising educational attainment and wider provision, the pressures of growth and diversification will probably shift some of the emphasis to the more advanced courses. This is often a gap in overall provision. A striking phenomenon in many countries is the concentration of young people in either general or in vocational education and the relatively low participation rates in long-cycle technical programmes (an exception being Italy, where of all upper secondary students, 44 per cent enrol in technical studies). It is also likely that the present sharp segmentation that frequently exists between academic and vocational studies is particularly restricting for the students of average levels of educational attainment. Among them, many seek alternatives to programmes that either lead directly to higher education or that are specifically job-related.

In designing the contents of post-compulsory programmes, the need for adequate preparation for work and employment has become a priority everywhere. At the same time, the drawbacks of acquiring overly specific occupational skills are repeatedly emphasized. Not only does narrow vocational preparation restrict the trainees' prospects, but the actual nature and content of their future work is very difficult to predict (see Chapter 3). How possible is it, therefore, to "train for uncertainty"? There seem to be three different approaches to this problem in OECD countries. The first is to broaden the initial training base: to group occupations in families, or to identify generic skills, so that the content of initial training becomes broader. With this "generic" approach, training can become progressively differentiated once the initial broad base is established. This is advocated in a number of countries, for example Finland[9]. It may be argued against it that it forces the youngster whose mind is already set on an occupation to learn much that appears to him or her superfluous as well as leaving those who do not pursue further specific training with an initial preparation that is too general.

A second approach is to shift the emphasis from *what* is learned to *how* it is learned – the process rather than the content. A "process" emphasis in training clearly holds out possibilities, but the problem is that it is difficult to find ways of translating abstract aims – such as those of transfer, learning to learn, or general problem-solving – into concrete operations. It demands a great deal from both students and teachers, who may often prefer to work in more concrete, routine fashion. A third approach is to retain existing specific initial training but to make provision for regular adult updating and retraining – the idea behind many of the arguments in favour of recurrent education. In some countries, this is an implicit part of their approach to training.

The "process" approach serves to underline (however difficult the approach itself may be to translate into concrete form) that questions of the curriculum extend beyond the *content* of studies. Indeed, it is at the post-compulsory level that most experimentation with the different main dimensions of the curriculum is taking place, for example, with the many schemes that combine work and study, whether in formal or less formal arrangements. Whatever the difficulties encountered in particular schemes, behind all these developments is the recognition that the learning environment is an important variable in curriculum policy for the 16-19 year-old age group. The content of studies does not exist in a vacuum and current preoccupations suggest, at the very least, that exposure to a variety of learning environments is considered important. Nor is it only the learning environment that affects students but the teaching-learning process and pedagogical practices. This is a complex area and one that involves a number of elements including role modelling, teaching styles, study habits and the hidden curriculum[10].

Whether the type of setting or combination of settings in which education takes place (in school or college, "dual" or non-formal) can succeed in blurring the present sharp dichotomies between general and vocational education or between education and training remains to be seen. In one way, the dual systems are more promising in this respect because of their broad coverage and because of their greater openness to less advantaged groups. At the same time, however, its main underlying principle is precisely the maintenance of two clearly separate sectors with contrasting values – one dominated by the academic ethos and the other by that of the workplace. But even greater difficulties of bridging the gap between education and training may be faced in countries where schooling is associated almost exclusively with general education, whether these countries follow a "schooling" or a "mixed" pattern of provision.

Thus one returns to the various measures and ideas that aim to "de-school" the upper secondary system to some degree. Several have been mentioned at various points throughout this chapter: the upgrading or development of certain vocational branches with a stronger academic basis, the more flexible combinations of work and study, the possible introduction of compulsory work experience into academic lines, the development of non-academic, general courses that are strongly geared to preparation for working life, the need to move away from "schools for children" for the 16-19 year-old age group towards more adult institutions that may also cater for older students in post-secondary education. Another avenue being explored involves the establishment of more direct links with the community, e.g. youth service, community colleges, and co-operative programmes of various types.

Though all of these may seek to blur certain rigid boundaries – between education and work, between schooling and training, and between education and the community – differentiation always emerges, and even increases, as described above. While this is a natural corollary of the diversity of students' interests and talents, it raises the serious problems of selection and inequality of opportunity. These have not been elaborated in this chapter since it is the focus of Chapter 4. It is important to underline, however, that the upper secondary stage of education and training is being assigned greater responsibility for the orientation, allocation and selection of students, increasingly postponed from the latter years of compulsory education. The differences between courses, programmes and institutions are not neutral concerning students' eventual chances in higher education and the labour market, and the hierarchies entailed may have become yet more sharp and distinct over recent years. And, as argued in Chapter 4, as more of the 16-19 year-old age group continue in post-compulsory education, those who drop out beforehand or who do not complete their course to acquire a qualification suffer still higher risk of stigma and social disadvantage. It is thus clear that a *sine qua non* of any policy aimed at enhancing the career and life-chances of those who have suffered from disadvantage or failure in education at an early stage is the provision and active promotion of recurrent opportunities within the post-compulsory education and training system.

NOTES AND REFERENCES

1. This chapter is based on the fuller analysis contained in *Education and Training after Basic Schooling,* OECD, Paris, 1985.

2. T. Husén, *The School in Question: A Comparative Study of the School and its Future in Western Societies,* Oxford University Press, pp. 130-131.

3. "Towards a Guarantee of Youth Opportunities", OECD/CERI, Paris, 1984 (document for general distribution).

4. With particular emphasis upon the labour market, see *New Policies for the Young,* OECD, Paris (forthcoming).

5. For a fuller discussion of main patterns of provision, see Chapter 2 of *Education and Training after Basic Schooling, op. cit.*

6. The figure of 87 per cent for the United States is made up of 81 per cent in secondary schools and 6 per cent in higher education. The breakdown in Canada is 60 per cent and 12 per cent in these two categories.

7. Manpower Services Commission, *New Training Initiatives: A Programme for Action,* London, 1981.

8. Already in the mid-1970s Coleman *et al.*'s report *(Youth: Transition to Adulthood. Report of the Panel on Youth of the President's Science Advisory Committee,* University of Chicago Press, 1974) drew attention to some of the dangers that result from a growing isolation of youngsters from adults and from increased differentiation of the young into narrowly-defined age groups.

9. *The Future of Vocational Education and Training,* OECD, Paris, 1983, pp. 24-38.

10. See *Education and Training after Basic Schooling, op. cit.,* Chapter 4.

Chapter 8

HIGHER EDUCATION AND THE NEEDS OF ADULTS

THE HIGHER EDUCATION SECTOR

As described in Chapter 2, OECD countries shared the very rapid expansion of higher education, especially during the 1960s and early 1970s. Few have escaped the slowdown in this growth that has been witnessed since then, even though most recently there have been signs of growing social demand for education at this level. The impact of economic recession and the related public questioning of the capacity of formal education to respond to new needs have been particularly pronounced at the higher education level. Financial restrictions and cutbacks are increasingly felt at a time when technological development and economic restructuring lay new and urgent responsibilities at the doors of the institutions of higher education. The expansion and diversification of higher education, and the closer links that have developed with the community and society it serves, have also brought a series of new roles, expectations and clienteles that are crucial to the development of policies for higher education in the 1980s. It is, thus, useful to view the further development of this sector by comparing these extended roles and new challenges with the strains in fulfilling its already established functions, especially with the pressures of constraint on public spending and confidence and the present difficult economic climate.

Generalisations concerning the present situation and future development of higher education are, however, fraught with special difficulties and for at least two main reasons. First, as concluded in the overview of issues in *Policies for Higher Education in the 1980s*[1], patterns of development are different among Member countries and may well become still more diverse in years to come:

"Already during the Golden Age of education, when most pressures converged in fostering rapid growth, countries coped with the advent of mass higher education in quite different ways. On the basis of the experience of the late 1970s and of the different national forecasts and policy statements, it would be reasonable to argue that the coming decades will witness a far greater diversity among Member countries in the patterns of development of their higher education systems" (p. 21).

Secondly, it is increasingly difficult and even misleading to talk of higher education as if it comprises a uniform sector. The courses and institutions of higher education are a complex and highly variegated array of opportunities, a direct corollary of expansion and diversification. They include long-cycle and short-cycle courses, catering for an increasingly diversified clientele, sometimes of highly specialised vocational purpose, sometimes with little direct application in the labour market. As will be discussed in more detail below, this complexity is becoming even more evident in the 1980s. For, whereas in the 1960s and the early years of the 1970s, the traditional university provided the dominant model and many expressed concern about the convergence of institutions in a process of "academic drift", this trend has, in many countries, been reversed. There is a tendency for short-cycle institutions to be less concerned with academic status and more with the immediate employment relevance of their courses while hierarchical differences *within* the university, as well as the non-university, sector have sharpened in recent years. This process has many implications and indeed risks, but it underlines the complexities of higher education systems and the difficulties of treating them as if they comprise a uniform sector.

Yet, in spite of national variations in the scope and form of higher education provision, and differences in institutional responses within and between countries, much of the pressure that is generating change is commonly felt, as are the challenges posed by new roles, expectations and clienteles.

THE RESPONSE TO DIVERSIFIED DEMAND
AND THE SPECIAL PLACE OF ADULTS

The Diversification of Demand for Higher Education

A central characteristic of higher education has always been its irreducible plurality of purposes which places it now under more severe strain than before. In addition to their traditional functions, universities and colleges are expected to perform a number of more explicit social and economic roles. These include: to respond to local and community demands, to contribute to the revitalisation of economies through the preparation of highly-qualified manpower and the further training of the workforce faced by rapid economic and technological change; to contribute to the maintenance of adequate levels of technological innovation through the advance of scientific knowlege; to sustain the move towards greater social equity, particularly at a time when economic difficulties hit hardest disadvantaged groups.

These widened purposes and expectations of higher education partly reflect, and are in part a response to, new and diversified demands from students as well as the wider community. One major way that new demands are felt by the institutions of higher education is in the growing importance attached to the immediate employment value of their courses and qualifications which has taken place alongside the deterioration, at least in absolute terms, of the labour market prospects of the graduates of higher education. Certain risks inherent in this trend need, however, to be underlined. The OECD report[1] presents them as follows:

"......in recognising the need to increase the employment relevance of many higher education programmes, governments and institutions should be fully aware of the dangers involved in adopting a too narrow or short-term employment perspective. Policies for higher education in the 1980s cannot ignore developments extending into the 1990s and beyond, which may entail drastic changes in the size and composition of the labour force and have very different implications for higher education."(p. 85)

The clear message is that there is a real danger that over-responsiveness to immediate pressures may undermine the capacity of higher education institutions to cope with longer-term needs and objectives.

The diversity of demand, however, does not spring only from the deteriorated labour market situation of the higher education graduates. It reflects also the needs of "new groups" or "non-traditional students". Particularly within universities, programmes have often been traditionally designed for the young, qualified student with the time and opportunity to pursue studies on a full-time basis, perhaps for several years. But the "non-traditional student" is now increasingly common. It is the young person looking to enter higher education on a part-time basis, combining studies with employment or other activities. In European countries especially, it is the young entrant from upper secondary vocational streams who previously was not allowed access to this level of education. It is the adult student, qualified or unqualified with the normal entrance requirements, who is entering higher education for a number of reasons. (The special place of adult demand is discussed in more detail below). Alternatively, the "non-traditional" student refers to sections of the population or social groups who previously were under-represented or largely absent from the programmes of higher education: women, students of low socio-economic status, ethnic minority students.

These different types of "new groups", who sometimes overlap and who do not all look for the same thing from higher education, illustrate the diversified nature of demand. In different ways, and to differing degrees, the higher education sector has responded. There has been a proliferation of shorter, specialised courses and the advent of more flexible modes of attendance. The numbers of part-time young students, for example, already commonplace in North America, are growing significantly elsewhere in OECD countries, especially in Europe. There are various forms of co-operative schemes and distance-learning arrangements. These developments have led to a blurring of the traditional boundaries between the formal and non-formal sectors of higher education provision and between higher and adult education. More open and flexible access to higher education has been a major aspiration of policies in this area over at least the last two decades. But it is the result, too, of the more recent response of institutions to the need to attract new resources and new clienteles in order to maintain their viability in the face of diminishing traditional student numbers and financial constraints.

These developments are not without their dangers. Some of these, particularly where institutions become over-responsive to short-term pressures at the expense of longer-term objectives, have already been pointed out. Some also fear, taking the example of the United States which is most advanced in the flexibility and diversity of its offering, that the increased competition for students may lead to practices of the market place that may even be questionable on ethical grounds[2]. But these developments can also be seen in the very positive light of change towards more open, flexible and democractic education and the stimulus of innovation, especially innovation at the institutional level.

Adult Demand and Continuing Education

There is evidence in many OECD countries that demand from, and participation by, adults in post-secondary education is significantly increasing. It is likely to constitute the main element of future growth at this level of education, and this is also of major qualitative significance. Some of the main factors behind this growth were described in Chapters 2 and 3: increased leisure with shorter working hours and longer periods of retirement, and greater periods of non-work enforced upon the individual by unemployment; increased opportunities for, and frequently the need of, career changes in mid-life; the obsolescence of knowledge and skills brought about by accelerated technological and social change; higher levels of initial education, conducive to continuing interest in education.

The purposes and motivations of adults who enter higher education are thus very varied and they can be categorised in simplified, schematic fashion in the following way:

a) Those who enter or re-enter higher education as adults in order to pursue mainstream studies leading to a full first degree or diploma ("delayers", "deferrers", or those who are admitted on credentials for work experience or second-chance educational routes);

b) Those who re-enter to up-date their professional knowledge, or seek to acquire additional qualifications, in order to change occupation or advance in their career ("refreshers", "recyclers");

c) Those without previous experience in higher education, who enrol for professional purposes especially in courses of short duration, though the boundaries between the "professional" and "general" may often not be very clear (e.g. in languages or computer sciences);

d) Those, with or without previous experience in higher education, who enrol for courses with the explicit purpose of personal fulfilment.

These different groups of adult learners comprise a sort of continuum between the "regular" higher education student and the "regular" adult education student. It is clear that, in many countries, institutions of adult education will continue to play an essential role in this field. But, as already seen, institutions of higher education have increasingly catered for "new" groups – adults prominent among them – and in some countries (as Germany and Sweden), this has been given additional impetus through national legislation stipulating that these institutions more closely respond to adult demand. Sweden has for several years operated the 25/4 entry scheme in higher education requiring a minimum age of 25 years and 4 years at least of working experience. Higher education establishments are potentially well placed, compared with their competitors in this field, to respond to the varied needs of adult students since they generally have highly-trained teachers, advanced technology and other facilities, as well as academic prestige.

There is, therefore, a growing proportion of adults in mainstream courses leading to recognised qualifications in many places. Where this does take place, it should affect profoundly the education offered to traditional students both in terms of curriculum and in the methodology and pedagogy of the learning process itself. The integration of adults into mainstream higher education is not the only alternative, however, as the OECD report[1] underlines:

"Perhaps of even greater significance, in terms of potential for the future, is the greater interest and efforts on the part of universities to provide in a more systematic way continuing education courses which respond to the specifically defined requirements of certain groups, e.g. short courses or special training schemes organised in co-operation with or under the sponsorship of professional groups, trade unions, enterprises, government agencies and other groups in the surrounding community." (p. 99)

It can thus be misleading to view the institutions of higher education as competing with these other bodies in meeting adult demand for education. In many cases, the task and challenge is precisely one of establishing networks of co-operation between them.

Still further removed from the principle of the integration of adults into mainstream provision is the creation of new specialised institutions with short or modular courses, part-time provision or distance learning. They may be aimed at a particular profession only (e.g. colleges of continuing education of teachers in Japan) or a particular age group (e.g. universités du troisième âge in France). One of the best known examples is the Open University in the United Kingdom, which combines distance learning with periodic on-site courses, and which was established exclusively for adults but has since extended its clientele to include younger students seeking alternatives to campus-based, full-time study. The Open

University has since been emulated in different forms in several other countries (Germany, Japan, Spain, the Netherlands). Another and longer-established example of distance learning for adults to acquire degrees on a part-time basis is the *Conservatoire national des Arts et Métiers* in France, which has 46 regional institutes as well as the central body in Paris. These different ways of meeting adult demand for education by institutions of higher education can and do take place simultaneously and are not mutually exclusive approaches. Even in countries where special "non-traditional" institutions have been set up, there is a growing disposition on the part of universities and colleges towards facilitating part-time attendance and developing schemes that allow for alternation between studies and work.

A major problem, that recurs throughout OECD countries, is the general tendency for those adults who already have a more extensive initial education to be those who most avail themselves of learning opportunities later in their lives. The evident danger is that existing educational inequalities will actually be widened through the development of continuing education, rather than narrowed. To some degree, it depends upon the kinds of adult students, and the measures to make courses more open, that are involved. "Second-chance" opportunities and the waiving of traditional entry qualifications allow certain students to acquire an education from which they otherwise would have been excluded. This is beneficial even if others who already have more education profit from widened learning opportunities for adults to an even greater degree. Not enough consideration, however, has been given to the pedagogical, financial and organisational arrangements that might, at the least, minimise the inequitable consequences of continuing education, if not actually reduce inequalities of educational opportunity. Making formal opportunities more equal between age groups is, therefore, no guarantee of greater social equity, and the two may even conflict. Experience from Sweden has revealed already some of the unintended consequences of favouring older qualified candidates. It can lead to the rejection of substantial numbers of young school leavers, often from less privileged groups, who may also find it increasingly difficult – with high levels of youth unemployment – to gain the work experience required by selective institutions of higher education.

Some of the inequalities in the participation in higher education of different sections of the population and social groups were described in Chapter 4. There has been much more progress in the enrolment of women than of students from lower social backgrounds or those from many ethnic and cultural minorities that generally suffer educational disadvantage. The female advance has been concentrated especially among women from more privileged social strata. Two additional reservations from Chapter 4 can be reiterated here. First, with the restrictions, and even contractions, in higher education in recent years, there are signs of a reversal in some of the gains that were made by under-represented groups during the last couple of decades. This applies particularly to the more prestigious programmes and establishments and those which appear to carry more risk for the student. This leads directly to the second reservation: namely, that despite the arrival of "new groups" in higher education, these are often concentrated in courses and institutions that either have declining employment value or lower academic prestige. Caution is thus required in concluding that the educational gap between the privileged and under-represented groups has narrowed – their relative positions have more often than not been maintained despite greater participation of the latter in certain sectors of higher education.

A further, more general, note of caution can be sounded concerning the implications for equality of opportunity of larger numbers of adults being integrated into the mainstream courses of higher education. It concerns the further entrenchment of the certifying and selective functions of education with the influx of adult students. That is, if many adults join the competitive chase after the diplomas of formal education then the development of recurrent education could add merely a further twist to the pressures already exerted by the credentials spiral – like another increase in the money supply fuelling inflation.

These credentialling risks are greater insofar as adults are admitted in larger numbers as "regular" students pursuing the courses and acquiring the qualifications of mainstream higher education. They apply less to adults on specialised short courses, and not at all for those who study for personal enjoyment and who do not use the education in question for entry or mobility in the job market. In addition, it can be suggested that the more usual does it become for adults to return to higher education, then the more important is the warning that adults who are likely to profit most from widened access to higher education are those who already have a more extensive initial education. As described in Chapter 4, the more embracing the process of certification and meritocracy, the further behind does it leave the least advantaged groups in society.

THE POSITION OF THE UNIVERSITIES

As stated at the outset, current and future developments in higher education can be illuminated by comparing the many roles it is expected to perform and the strains now apparent in meeting them. This applies particularly to universities, since they are expected to maintain high levels of teaching and research while catering for a broadened and diverse demand. As many establishments in the non-university sector increasingly find their identity by catering for the new clientele, often by provision of visible employment value, and as the traditional university model loses some of its attraction and prestige, it is now the university sector that can be regarded as deserving special concern.

One of the most tangible sources of concern for universities in many countries are resources. Budgetary cuts, however justified by immediate financial considerations and whatever their stimulus to greater efficiency, have long-term consequences. The quality of learning resources can be seriously affected. Faculties that are regarded as more marginal or less useful in job terms are being increasingly squeezed. Capital equipment is becoming obsolete leading to the concern that students are being inadequately prepared with modern, up-to-date skills, methods and techniques. There is often a lack of new blood, an ageing of faculty members, with little staff mobility or openings. Restrictions on resources are felt throughout the universities in most countries, one crucial area being research.

A central function of the university, which often distinguishes it from other post-secondary institutions, is its pursuit of knowledge through research. In addition to its influence on the quality of teaching, university research has an important impact on the success of other applied research and on technological and industrial development. Within national systems of research, the part universities play varies from country to country. In some cases, universities are *the* locus of public research. They face a complex of demands upon their capacities, ranging from engagement in the most sophisticated scientific research to problem-solving for small local firms. The legitimate claim that this should serve a wide audience does not mean that whole areas of research should be jeopardised by over-responsiveness to external requirements. These requirements are felt in several ways. One of the most direct is the growing importance of external funds in some countries (from research councils, ministries, private industry) as sources of support, and these sources, correspondingly, exercise influence upon the scale and direction of university research. Disparities between disciplines grow as the social sciences and, still more, the humanities find it hard to compete with the "hard" sciences in demonstrating their immediate usefulness.

The ability of the university to remain a centre of excellence in teaching and research thus returns in part to the question of how far it can, or is allowed to, strike a balance between short-term needs and long-term objectives. But more specifically, it concerns the nature of control and decision-making. The arguments that universities have in the past been insufficiently accountable for their high financial costs and that academic freedom has too often meant academic isolation have considerable validity. Yet, in becoming more accountable and responsible, will their special status in society be preserved? And is society, to which they become more accountable, sufficiently clear about the objectives it wishes universities to serve or will it place upon them an impossible burden of demands, some of which will necessarily remain unfulfilled?

FUTURE POLICY OPTIONS AND DILEMMAS

The overall size of higher education provision no longer depends, as it once seemed, upon the social demand of the traditional student age group. Nor, concerning the structure of higher education, is there the same support for comprehensive institutions and the gradual integration of different types and levels of programme. The relatively neat models and guidelines have become blurred and complex. In this context, present policies and future options for the development of higher education are presented with a series of related paradoxes. On the one hand, policies no longer adhere to the "demand-led" principle (exemplified by the 1960s Robbins report in the United Kingdom). On the other hand, institutions are more than ever dependent for their survival upon meeting the demands of diverse groups of students, some as yet untapped. On the one hand, higher education as a whole is less shaped and structured by central educational planning. On the other hand, the factor of supply, and hence of policy influence, in determining the size and structure of provision has become greater, especially with the curtailment of resources. On the one hand, higher education is more influenced by, and accountable to, external forces, including governments. On the other, the criteria and objectives by which the institutions of higher education know they are being assessed, to the extent that they are becoming more visible and explicit, are not necessarily those that the institutions themselves would consider relevant.

The major choices these paradoxes highlight pull in conflicting directions. They suggest that central policy guidance for higher education should become firmer in order that expectations and objectives become more visible and clear, in order that excellence in teaching and research be assured and "soft" subjects be not unduly pared and downgraded, in order that, more generally, long-term objectives are defined and safeguarded. Yet, alongside this must be recognition that, in this and future decades, many groups and interests that are external to educational institutions and administrations are intimately involved in the educational process – as clients, as providers of education, and as decision-makers. This is taking place throughout education but is perhaps most sharply felt at the higher education level. The question raised then is: How can a coherent policy planning process for the higher education sector be instituted when the traditional policy bodies and instruments hold still less of a monopoly of decision-making than they did before?

It has further to be recognised that policy planning for higher education in the coming decades has to reconcile the two interrelated functions of higher education systems which have been brought out in this chapter: the provision of high-level initial training for the professions and the production and dissemination of new knowledge on the one hand, and, on the other,

91

the provision of a wide range of formal and less formal specialised programmes in response to a broad demand including that of adults and non-traditional students. It is already possible to discern an increasing polarisation of policy approaches in response to these two functions – a more or less controlled and selective approach implying a relatively protected environment for the former; greater openness and flexibility geared to demand-oriented provision for the latter. In part, it reflects the changing hierarchies among courses and institutions, which are themselves the result of the changing preferences of the student population. With the shift in the weight attached to academic versus employment value, there has been a change in the "pecking order" of institutions and disciplines that partly reflects conscious government policies and choices about the distribution of more limited public funds within higher education.

At the institutional level, this gives rise to problems that are felt acutely by those establishments that occupy an intermediary position between the élite universities and their equivalents, on the one side, and the professionally-oriented, short-cycle institutions, on the other. They have special difficulties in maintaining their competitive position and defining their future role. Should they strengthen their academic objectives, become liberal arts colleges, or else move towards being more vocationally-oriented institutions?

At the faculty level, the social sciences and humanities suffer particular vulnerability. They expanded enormously throughout the 1960s and 1970s but since then, the job markets that their graduates entered, particularly teaching and the public services, have severely contracted and their "usefulness" is questioned. The relevance of these subjects in broadly-based higher education courses, including technological programmes, can easily be overlooked. These more vulnerable courses and programmes tend to be those that are open and unselective in contrast with others, more prestigious or sought-after, that are often selective and are better protected. The former will tend to contain more from the "new groups" and have higher rates of drop-out and non-completion (though this in itself is not necessarily negative, as for some it is deliberate and chosen). The latter programmes are likely to cater for the more privileged, qualified, traditional student.

The tendency may thus be for courses and institutions to become increasingly polarised. To some degree, this is positive and permits specialisation and a greater concentration of function. It may, in any event, be a reality that countries will have to come to terms with as they face the future. But the dangers are also clear. In particular, it could well reinforce segregation among higher education institutions and the social inequities that already afflict higher education. And it could threaten the more open courses and programmes with constant uncertainty, instability and possible downgrading of staff and resources. Not all countries will share the same path of development and the diversity among countries could well become more marked in the future. But now, perhaps, the time is ripe for a full and positive assessment of what is expected of higher education and of each of its constituent institutions, as well as the means that are required to realise these expectations in the years to come.

NOTES AND REFERENCES

1. *Policies for Higher Education in the 1980s,* OECD, Paris, 1983.
2. See *Fair Practices in Higher Education,* A Report of the Carnegie Council on Policy Studies on Higher Education, Jossey-Bass, San Francisco, 1979.

Chapter 9

EXPENDITURE AND FINANCING: TRENDS AND ISSUES

PATTERNS OF EDUCATIONAL EXPENDITURE

The Overall Picture: Public and Other Forms of Educational Spending

Certain of the global trends in public educational expenditure were outlined in Chapter 2[1]. There, it was seen that the general picture is one where education's share of the growing affluence and resources of Member countries grew during the 1960s and into the 1970s but has since declined; while as a proportion of social expenditure, education, contrary to its position twenty years ago, is now behind both health and, especially, pensions[2]. In real terms, several countries (Canada, Italy, Sweden, New Zealand) experienced their first actual decline in educational expenditure in the early 1970s before returning to positive growth. The latter years of the last decade and the early 1980s again witnessed years of a real fall in educational spending in several countries (Australia, Canada, the Netherlands, the United Kingdom, New Zealand).

The variations between Member countries are far from insignificant. In 1980 education's part of public expenditure stood in percentage terms at 16, 17 or more in some countries (Australia, Japan, the United States), compared with 11-12 per cent or less elsewhere (Austria, Germany, the Netherlands, New Zealand). Since such magnitudes cannot form the basis of meaningful comparisons between countries, it is more revealing to look at trends within each one. In so doing, the decline in educational spending since the mid-1970s should not be exaggerated. The previous period had, after all, been one of extraordinary financial expansion even if enrolments in schools were already falling in the 1970s, markedly so in some countries. And in Italy, education's share of GDP in real terms still continued to rise into the 1980s as it did in Ireland and Belgium. In Germany, Austria and Sweden, education's portion of GDP fell during the latter years of the 1970s only very slightly, if at all.

Figures at this level of aggregation, however, give only a very approximate picture of the nature of educational spending and they do not indicate which elements of education received more or fewer resources, especially for the most recent years for which data are frequently absent. Nor do they show the often significant sums of money that are not counted in the budgets of public educational expenditure, even though they are directed to activities with a major educational component. Even a single non-formal programme, the Youth Training Scheme recently implemented in the United Kingdom, cost some £1 000 million in its first year (1982/83) of operation. Whether more or less is now being spent on non-formal educational programmes is extremely difficult to establish, partly because the necessary

93

evidence is lacking, partly because it refers to such an ill-defined, diverse category of learning activities. In the United Kingdom, expenditure on work preparation and experience programmes nearly tripled between 1974/75 and 1980/81, rising from the equivalent of 9 per cent of total expenditure on formal education to 11 per cent at the beginning of this decade. In Canada, on the other hand, the share of spending on education devoted to vocational training fell between 1976 and 1981[3]. In Italy, the Ministry of Public Education increased its share of the total, which includes the educational spending of several other ministries, from 82.8 per cent in 1976 to 87.5 per cent in 1980. In these cases, then, spending on non-formal programmes may have fallen.

With such widely varying scope and meaning of "non-formal", and with figures showing diverging trends, no clear indication of the changing status of these programmes can be made here. Greater clarification of the dimension and components of this area would, however, be very useful to overall policy-making, as the boundaries between education and training and between formal and non-formal sectors become increasingly blurred and as it becomes more necessary to consider available learning opportunities as a whole, especially those for adolescents and adults.

Private expenditure on education, the size of which in some countries is substantial, is another area where a clear picture is difficult to establish. By no means all private education in Member countries is, in fact, funded from non-public sources. In several (as France, Finland, Luxembourg, the Netherlands, Spain, Switzerland, Germany), private schools receive substantial amounts of income from the public sector. This may take the form, as in France, of payment of teachers' salaries, or through the payment of capital grants and/or subsidies towards operating costs. In considering expenditure on education that is strictly private, a distinction can be made at least between private inputs into the direct costs of running and operating schools and colleges (for example, in the form of tuition fees) and household expenditures devoted to education that can remain largely hidden but which can be very significant (though the two overlap).

Concerning the former, the relative importance of private expenditure may well have fallen in countries, as public authorities have taken on a greater number of responsibilities that previously were left in private hands. This could be reversed, however, if there are increasing moves towards privatisation. When household expenditure is considered, there is evidence that private spending on education has risen in many countries and may now be substantial. It has been estimated that private household expenditure on education in the United Kingdom almost doubled in real terms over the 1960s and 1970s, representing some 0.5 per cent of GNP in 1981. This amounted to about £1 000 million. The Japanese figure seems to be considerably higher. It has been estimated that total expenditure by households on education was nearly 3 per cent of national income in 1980. And in the United States, corporate and foundation contributions are rising substantially, and reached approximately 5 billion dollars in 1981.

Capital Expenditures and Educational Facilities

Compared with current expenditures, those spent on educational capital formation are now generally only a small part of the total. Since a substantial proportion of current expenditure is devoted to the salaries of teachers and other personnel, that are relatively fixed and difficult to reduce at least in the short-term, and since this proportion tends to grow because of the ageing of the teaching force, a general reaction throughout Member countries has been to cut capital spending, in some cases, radically. It is certainly implausible to argue that cuts on the scale that have been implemented in some countries have not affected the quality of educational provision, and this issue could well loom increasingly in the future as present buildings and facilities age and wear out.

In many countries, capital expenditure is no higher than one-tenth of total educational spending. In Belgium, France, Greece, the United Kingdom, and the United States, it had fallen to as low as 4-6 per cent of the total by 1978/80. In 1982, it was still no higher than 4 per cent in France. The fall is a marked one since around a fifth to a quarter of spending was devoted to investment at the beginning of the 1970s in many countries, when facilities were still being expanded to accommodate growing numbers of pupils and students. The proportion of expenditure directed to capital formation is not everywhere as low as the examples mentioned above. In Yugoslavia, Austria, Portugal and Ireland it stands between 13-16 per cent. The proportion of expenditure devoted to capital formation remained consistently high in Japan throughout the 1970s and still stands at about 25 per cent – significantly higher than in the other countries for which the OECD has data.

With the common pattern of school systems facing falling rolls, it may be regarded as natural that educational capital investments did not maintain the same pace as prevailed previously under contrary circumstances. Many schools now face the problem of rapidly rising per-capita costs. However, the concept of "surplus" that this implies, and the meaning of per-capita costs themselves, are far from fixed and clearcut. While a growing number of schools may be underutilised in relation to current norms and expectations, and hence be said to exhibit surplus, there is always the need for qualitative improvements, for better accommodation when much of the existing school stock is clearly inadequate and ageing, and for provision that meets new demands. Equally, per-capita costs would alter considerably if school buildings were more efficiently used to respond to other groups in the population and to meet the needs of the wider community. Many countries have in fact sought to improve the efficiency of school premises by broadening their purpose and encouraging their use by groups other than the fixed school population and at times other than just during school hours and the weeks of the regular semester. Apart from the fact that many educational buildings are out-dated and inadequate, and that new needs and uses arise, there is the additional consideration that the common trend of falling enrolments in schools cannot be assumed to be a permanent one. Enrolment fluctuation rather than steady decline, albeit fluctuation within plausible limits, becomes then the appropriate planning guide.

As educational capital formation falls to very low levels in many countries, and as reductions in spending on the maintenance of facilities has appeared a less painful way of implementing expenditure cuts, serious problems may well arise in the future. Concerning maintenance of existing stock and facilities, let alone new investments, it is not exaggerated to say that from almost any viewpoint, the maintenance backlog problem seems to be approaching crisis proportions. On the one hand, there is accumulating and ageing building stock with escalating need for recurrent expenditure. On the other hand, there are such limits to the availability of both capital and recurrent funds that authorities are now frequently falling seriously behind in their maintenance programmes.

Expenditures in the Different Levels and Sectors of Education

Given the changing patterns of enrolments between educational sectors and certain shifts of priorities that have been described in the previous chapters, a redistribution of expenditures from one level to another could have been expected. In several countries, such a redistribution did take place. However, it did not fully follow the direction that might have been predicted on the basis of enrolments or numbers in the different age groups. Some countries maintained the share directed to primary and secondary schools as enrolments declined, or else reduced it less than the fall in rolls, hence leading to a higher rate of growth of per-pupil expenditure in these sectors than in further and higher education. In several countries, the share of expenditure allotted to higher education actually fell, despite the increasing numbers in the appropriate age groups. Policy priority areas, such as pre-primary schooling and vocational/technical education, have tended to do well relative to other sectors. There are, of course, exceptions. Japan, for example, maintained a very even balance in growth of per-capita expenditure across the different educational levels both in the period 1970-75 (though higher education per-student expenditure growth lagged slightly behind the other levels at this time) and since.

The declining relative fortunes of universities and higher education are seen in the Netherlands (universities received 21.2 per cent of total expenditure in 1970, 18.3 per cent in 1975 and 18.1 per cent in 1980)[4]; Australia (the universities received 16.1 per cent in 1971/72, 14.8 per cent in 1976/77, 13.1 per cent in 1980/81)[5]; France for higher education as a whole (15.5 per cent in 1967, 14.0 per cent in 1977, 11.9 per cent in 1982 and 12.2 per cent in 1983); and England and Wales (12.0 per cent in 1970/71, 9.5 per cent in 1975/76, rising slightly to 10.2 per cent in 1979/80).

In Germany, the proportion of the total share allocated to higher education stayed fairly constant (24.9 per cent in 1970, 23.9 per cent in 1975, 22.9 per cent in 1980, 23.3 per cent in 1982). In terms of per-student growth rates of expenditure, however, higher education fared much less well than the other levels. Annual per-student growth rates of 7 per cent in primary schools, 3.8 per cent in the *Realschulen,* 4.3 per cent in the *Gymnasium* and 6.8 per cent in technical and vocational education between 1975 and 1980, compare with only 0.3 per cent in higher education. If per-student expenditures are examined, rather than the absolute share as above, then the declining relative position of higher education in resource terms in the United Kingdom is more marked still. In Canada and the United States, higher education has maintained its standing relative to other sectors in the resources it receives. [In Canada, it was 26.9 per cent in 1976 and 27.2 per cent in 1981-82[3]; in the United States, 35.0 per cent in 1969/70, 35.1 per cent in 1975/76, 36.0 per cent in 1979/80[6]]. Because of falling enrolments in primary and secondary education and increasing numbers in higher education, however, higher education experienced lower annual per-student expenditure growth rates than those enjoyed by the schools in these countries too.

In contrast, schools have fared relatively well. Despite the common pattern of declining enrolment rates, their share of total resources were either maintained or they fell less than the corresponding drop in pupil numbers. The general trend towards lower teacher/pupil ratios has already been mentioned in Chapter 2, one concrete indicator of the improved relative position of schools. The high priority given to vocational education and training and, in some countries, pre-primary education has been reflected in their receipt of public funds, as the following examples show. The share of total current expenditure directed to TAFE (Technical and Further Education) in Australia rose through the years between 1971/72 and 1980/81. Standing at 6.5 per cent at the beginning of this period, it reached 9.4 per cent by the end. As seen above, per-student expenditure in vocational branches in Germany grew rapidly compared with most other sectors. And in Italy, the vocational and technical branches of upper secondary education experienced a significantly higher growth of resources in real terms than did compulsory schooling, general upper secondary education or universities. Similarly, large sums of money have been made available in countries such as the United Kingdom for work experience and training programmes. Much the greatest increase in Italy, however, was seen in pre-primary education: between 1971 and 1980, expenditure in real terms increased by 286 per cent. Per-pupil expenditure growth rates in the Netherlands were higher for pre-primary provision than for any other sector.

Based on only a limited number of countries, the picture painted above can only be illustrative of certain apparent trends, though these are in line with the patterns of priorities identified in previous chapters. To what extent this is actually reflected in conscious policies for the redeployment of resources between sectors, and how effective such policies have been, is by no means clear-cut. As emphasized above, much remains to be done in making facilities and staff more flexible in their use and thus the total stock of educational resources more efficient. But, equally, it is clear that some redeployment has taken place. The fact that certain countries have increased teacher/pupil ratios in sectors that have suffered falling enrolments is consistent with the widespread aim of improving quality, particularly the quality of basic schooling. It can be argued, in addition, that since higher education had fared so well in the 1960s and early 1970s, and is a much more expensive sector than schools, it was only to be expected that it should feel the effect of constraints to a greater degree. In actual practice, of course, it may well be that governments have found it politically easier to cut back on students, staff and facilities in higher education rather than reduce teacher costs at the school level, strongly defended by a well-organised teaching profession.

ISSUES OF FINANCING

No OECD country seriously questions the public service nature of its educational provision, essentially publicly financed. But systems for financing education differ widely not only from one country to another but also within countries, especially between the different levels of education. No single "best" financing system exists since they can only be assessed in relation to the different aims of education which immediately raises the question of priorities[7]. It is thus difficult to discuss financing systems in general terms and only a small number of the more prominent issues can be taken up here.

A principal issue for the future is how the sources of educational finance can be broadened. With the increased difficulty facing governments trying to raise general tax finance, any system heavily dependent upon central government grant finance is going to come under pressure. This suggests the need to investigate the scope for developing alternative sources of finance. Most systems retain important elements of local public finance but local governments may also be expected to experience difficulties in raising adequate levels of revenue in a political climate in which there is increased aversion on the part of households and firms to provide non-earmarked, general tax revenue.

Because of this, the scope for drawing upon private sources of finance is increasingly considered. Already, as has been noted, households are spending large, and sometimes considerable, sums that do not appear in the normal budgetary estimates of educational expenditure. In some countries, a growing portion of educational support is in the form of donated equipment, materials and services. Some measure of privatisation may enhance community involvement and may promote provision that either does not at present exist or where present facilities are inadequate. Yet the dangers are well known. Not only can greater reliance on private revenues exacerbate inequalities of provision from one area to another; it can also widen inequalities between groups and individuals to the extent that educational opportunity becomes more dependent upon the "ability to pay". This was raised in Chapter 7 in relation to the United States and Japan, where it was argued that the opportunity for parents to supplement existing public education through resort to the private sector has increased differentiation among students and schools.

97

It is important in this context to distinguish between levels and types of education. The issues raised by private financing for compulsory schooling, which seeks to ensure acceptable standards for all, are clearly different from those concerning higher or adult education where attendance is not compulsory, where certain aspects of education can be interpreted in "consumption" terms, and where many students possess some ability to pay. Considering appropriate financing systems for each level of education, however, goes well beyond the specific questions related to private revenues.

The OECD report on financing primary schools concluded that "the search for a 'perfect' or 'ideal' system of school finance is likely not only to be unnecessary, but futile[8]." Different systems can achieve similar results; for example, it concludes that unitary states do not necessarily achieve greater equalisation than federal countries, nor does a more uniform structure imply greater neglect of local autonomy. But the report does conclude that, in the latter case, it makes a significant difference how the non-local funds are made available. Equally, these questions cannot be resolved except by reference to the goals and priorities being pursued and hence they are also essentially political. Clearly, one major goal is equalisation of resources to schools and pupils. In many countries, there are marked differences between the per-pupil expenditures from one administrative area to another (which can hide further divergences within areas). To take but one example, in the United States, expenditure per pupil in schools varies between the states from $1 741 in Alabama in 1979/80 to $3 681 in New York State (and $5 146 in Alaska)[9]. Equal financial inputs do not necessarily mean equal outcomes. Some countries, in fact, recognise the need to discriminate in favour of schools in disadvantaged localities in order to maintain the standards enjoyed by those in well-provided areas. Per-pupil expenditure in certain sparsely populated areas in a number of countries are considerably higher than in urban areas.

In higher education, two important areas in financing are tuition costs and systems of student support. Systems for financing tuition could hardly be more diverse:

"At present, fees are charged in higher education institutions in Canada, Japan, the United Kingdom, the United States, but are mostly non-existent in Continental Europe and in Australia although the latter government has just announced its intention to introduce fees for post-graduate study. The proportion of income derived from fees and private donations varies considerably between countries and institutions."[10]

One issue that has been much discussed is the degree to which government subsidies to higher education should be channelled through individuals or institutions. In the United Kingdom, the increase in tuition fees that occurred around 1978 affected most individual students minimally (home students at least) since these fees are normally paid in full by local education authorities. Hence, the increase was largely only a transfer of direction of part of the public subsidy of higher education from institutions to individuals. Complex questions of efficiency and equity are raised by the issue of individual versus institutional subsidies. Some have linked this to a more general system of vouchers, arguing that the public subsidy should take the form of individual entitlements that could be used by adults of all ages in order to choose both where and when they pursue post-secondary education[11]. Allusion to the risks inherent in strengthening the market nature of higher education that this might imply, has already been made in Chapter 8. It can also be said that a system of individual entitlements would be highly inequitable if made available only to some and not to others. Yet, if all were to take up their rights under a generalised entitlement system, it is likely that either the overall cost of higher education would rise significantly, at a time when countries are seeking constraints or cutbacks, or else the level of each entitlement would have to be set so low that it would not be sufficient to enable all students to pursue the studies of their choice.

In whichever way the public subsidy to higher education is distributed, in all countries it involves some transfer from the general taxpayer to students who tend to come from the more privileged strata of society. This can be contested on equity grounds. Yet it is, perhaps, a certain price that society should be willing to pay in order to preserve the special status and value of higher education in Member countries.

Equity questions are also central to consideration of student aid. In most countries, one of the main objectives of student aid is to ensure that poor students are not prevented from entering or continuing in higher education through their inability to meet living expenses. Again, there is the widest variety of practices in Member countries in their student support schemes – whether they are made as grants or loans, whether they cover all (or nearly all) students or are selective, whether their level is based on parental income or the student's own, the terms on which loans have to be repaid, whether student support is direct or else indirectly paid through subsidy to other items such as food or housing. There has been some discussion and experimentation with the alteration of these various components and terms between students in order to make particular subjects or branches more attractive. The general trend in OECD countries, however, is towards more egalitarian systems of student aid, which treat students equally, regardless of the subject they study or the occupation they hope to enter.

It has been shown in Sweden that use of the national financial aid system is clearly related to the successful completion of studies and that this is most apparent among students from the lowest socio-economic backgrounds[12]. This provides a further nuance to the general argument that the public financing of higher education is inequitable because the public as a whole subsidises students who tend to be drawn predominantly from more privileged socio-economic classes. The more pertinent equity issue is, perhaps, how this subsidy can be used to encourage the maximum number of less privileged young people to enter higher education, as well as the older adults who are taxpayers as part of "second-chance" opportunities of continuing education.

A more evident inequitable anomaly within education is not that higher education is supported by taxpayers, many of whom are unable to profit from it, but that most countries devote far more financial aid to students in universities or other higher education institutions than to those in upper secondary education. As expressed by the OECD Higher Education report:

"Several countries now recognise that even though their policies on secondary school selection and admission are designed to extend educational opportunities, this is not sufficient to secure equality of opportunity when there are strong financial incentives persuading pupils from low-income families to leave school at the minimum age."[13]

It has been shown in the United Kingdom how the cost of maintaining a young person at school beyond the statutory leaving age, especially that borne by parents, is much higher than maintaining a university student[14].

Whatever the particular system of aid in place in each country, significant differences exist in the financial situation of those in the different levels of education as well as between those in education and training and young people who are employed or unemployed. It is frequently maintained that the relative levels of educational allowances (where they exist) and unemployment compensation must be set so that no young person is penalised for continuing in education and training. However, since direct educational allowances for post-compulsory students who are not in higher education are low or do not exist in most countries, this would seem tantamount to proposing the reduction of unemployment benefits to unacceptably low levels, penalising, in this case, the young person who prefers to be in the labour market but who cannot find a job. In some countries, for example Australia, there is considerable interest in examining these issues with the view that personal finance is a crucial variable in educational and early labour market decisions. It is certainly clear that the financial element is an important one in the implementation of the concept of a youth guarantee, however interpreted. But more generally, there is the need to give serious coordinated attention to the situation and financial support of young people in upper secondary school, those out of work and those in higher education.

NOTES AND REFERENCES

1. As in Chapter 2, the main sources of empirical data for this chapter are *Resource Redeployment in Education,* OECD, Paris (forthcoming) and *Educational Trends in the 1970s: A Quantitative Analysis,* OECD, Paris, 1984.

2. *Social Expenditure 1960-1990: Problems of Growth and Control,* OECD, Paris, 1985.

3. Statistics Canada, *Financial Statistics of Education 1980-81,* No. 81-208, Chart 2.

4. *Zakboek Onderwijsstatistieken, 1983,* CBS, The Hague, p. 118.

5. G. Burke, "Public Educational Expenditure in the 1970s and 1980s", in *The Australian Economic Review,* 3rd Quarter, 1983, p. 39.

6. *Digest of Education Statistics,* National Center for Education Statistics Washington, D.C., 1977/78, Table 19; and 1982, Table 15.

7. See *Educational Financing and Policy Goals for Primary Schools: General Report and Country Studies,* OECD/CERI, Paris, 1979.

8. *Educational Financing and Policy Goals for Primary Schools: General Report, op. cit.,* p. 66.

9. *Digest of Education Statistics 1982.* National Center for Education, Washington, D.C., Table 71.

10. *Policies for Higher Education in the 1980s,* OECD, Paris, 1983, pp. 191-192.

11. H. M. Levin, "Individual Entitlements" in H. M. Levin and H. G. Schütze (eds.), *Financing Recurrent Education: Stategies for Increasing Employment, Job Opportunities, and Productivity,* Sage, Beverly Hills, London, New Delhi, 1983.

12. S. E. Reuterberg and A. Svensson, "The Importance of Financial Aid: The Case of Higher Education in Sweden", *Higher Education,* Vol. 12, 1983.

13. *Policies for Higher Education in the 1980s, op. cit.,* p. 198.

14. D. Piachaud, "The Economics of Educational Opportunity", in *Higher Education,* Vol. 4, 1975.

Part Four

OVERVIEW AND CONCLUSIONS

OVERVIEW AND CONCLUSIONS

This report has taken as fundamental the reality that education must be responsive to, and play a full part in, the changing social and economic conditions of today's world. But it has also emphasized repeatedly the need to protect schools against the fluctuating swings of educational fashion and to safeguard their long-term missions against the buffeting of short-term pressures. In particular, it stresses that the clear responsibility of educational policy to play its part when labour market pressures and unemployment are high should not be interpreted as the requirement to re-write curricula and re-order priorities around the sole criterion of immediate employment "relevance".

The need to find this balance emerges across all the sectors of education as analysed in Chapters 6 to 8 (those on compulsory, post-compulsory and higher education). In each, greater community involvement in education is called for, as are new relations between general education and vocational preparation and a more active role in, and awareness of, technological development by the education systems of OECD countries. Each of these requirements necessitates that schools and colleges open their doors more fully to clienteles and interests that traditionally have been regarded as external to the institutions of education. Yet, this should not be interpreted as a diversion from their principal educational tasks. Schools are centres of learning preparing all young people for adult life and this should not be diluted by a multitude of further social tasks that, at most, are only partially the school's responsibility. Regarding higher education, the danger is perceived that whole areas of knowledge, particularly in the "soft" subjects of social sciences and humanities, as well as the vital contribution of research, might be unduly pared and reduced because their employment relevance is perceived as less than immediate. Neither the social understanding of technological change and its use, for example, nor the creative use of greater non-work and leisure time can be fully realised without the perception that derives from the human sciences, the arts, and the humanities. The learning needs of contemporary societies cannot be reduced to narrow specialisms.

This report has drawn attention to the extensive demands which are now made upon education, with pressures pulling in many, sometimes conflicting, directions, coinciding with a period of financial constraints as many Member countries seek to limit the calls upon the public purse. This gives rise to the fundamental questions: "Is too much being expected of education? Is too much being loaded at its door?".

Steering a meaningful course through the manifold expectations that confront education will require clarification of the nature of the learning society desired in each Member country and of what "education", in all its forms and settings, means in the modern world and what its principal goals are. No less important is the need to clarify the specific responsibilities of the different institutions and sectors that make up the formal education system and their special contribution to education in its broadest sense.

The need for such clarification also arises because the scope of education has broadened considerably over the last two decades. A wide array of organised learning opportunities now are set in non-formal locations outside the formal education system, including enterprises. The modes of attendance of students have greatly diversified, as Chapters 7 and 8 underline. Part-time study, "alternation" between education and other activities, distance learning have become the norm for many students. "Education" clearly is no longer synonymous with "what goes on in schools". In other words, the speed of social and education change has outstripped the vocabulary and concepts we use to describe and think about them.

This report has aimed to stimulate the search for new definitions and concepts and has suggested some of the most pertinent considerations in doing this. It recognises that in such a clarification there is no one-best, single model of educational organisation which could fit all the OECD countries, with their rich variety of culture and society, history and development. It also recognises that in each country the clarification of the scope and purpose of education will involve all groups in the community which it serves. It involves the social partners, who often disagree about priorities and the means to achieve the basic goals, which includes the need for clearer signals from employers concerning what they expect from education. Different government departments, as well as levels of administration, will be involved as will education's main clientele – students – who become more diverse and socially representative the more that education becomes available to all citizens throughout their lives. It must, therefore, ultimately take place through a process of social dialogue and participation, with the disagreement and conflict, as well as consensus, that this implies.

The contrasting themes of *continuity* and *change* predominate the analysis of the social and economic phenomena addressed in Part Two of this report, and their broad educational implications as well as more specific responses, as covered in Part Three.

The *continuity* of the basic educational goals and the need to safeguard good practice and institutions of proven quality stand out in a world so typified by change. This can be illustrated by several of the main conclusions of the report. Changing socio-economic conditions have not altered the need for basic school education for all young people to be of the highest quality, which depends upon the quality of the teaching force being equally maintained at the highest professional standards. Despite the flourishing new initiatives and innovations at the post-compulsory level of education and training, many outside the formal system, it has been shown in Chapter 7 that the formal upper secondary school or college remains the principal learning setting for young people above school leaving age in the majority of OECD countries and, indeed, this is becoming more pronounced in several. Equally for higher education, the report has sought to emphasize that the requirement to respond to the widening diversity of student demands must not be at the expense of traditional functions, such as research, nor of a balanced curriculum of offerings that includes the arts and the humanities as much as the economically "relevant". It has also placed special emphasis upon the long-standing objective of realising greater equity in education and of giving particular priority to low-achievers and disadvantaged groups. This remains as important as ever despite the changing conditions of recent years.

There are important aspects of continuity in education's socio-economic environment too, even though its change has been the subject of much of this report. In this regard, it should be noted that the socio-economic inequalities of income and occupation are extremely resilient to change and that education systems in all countries play an integral part in the process of social selection – to a greater or lesser degree. Furthermore, despite the progress made by education in combating socio-economic inequalities, it still comes up against the "iron law" described in Chapter 4, whereby privileged groups adopt strategies to safeguard that privilege. These can be explicit, such as actually moving house and neighbourhood, thus maintaining the social exclusivity of their children's schooling. Or they can be less conscious, as happens when the pressures of credentialism redefine and upgrade the "target" of sought-after educational courses and certificates out of reach of the less privileged once they have gained access to lower levels.

In Chapter 4, it is emphasized that this detracts nothing from the requirement of education policy to strive to achieve greater equality of opportunity and to combat the plight of the low-achiever. But since the social pressures that operate to maintain selectivity are extensive and deep-seated, and since the current labour market situation exacerbates critically the disadvantage of low-achievement, it suggests that the way forward towards greater equality of opportunity must come through the concerted action of radical educational policies that cover all levels and settings. Under-achievement should be identified and tackled as early as possible and in basic schooling new approaches and curricular and pedagogical practices are needed in order that each might acquire a sound basis of knowledge and skills as well as the appetite for further learning. These are certain to involve close co-operation within the community and will place particular demands on teachers, which will often require special training. But their effectiveness will be much reduced if they are not supported by policies that allow further education periodically through the life-cycle, starting with "second-chance" opportunities for secondary-level qualifications in the post-compulsory sector, and continuing with provision for professional training and retraining and for the many activities (leisure, self-care, community activity, political participation) further removed from the job market.

While continuity is thus apparent in certain major trends and aims, *change* is the striking feature of today's world. Education systems have had to confront rapidly falling pupil rolls which will continue in many countries and affect secondary and post-secondary education to a growing extent. They have witnessed a burgeoning participation of girls and women in many programmes in schools, colleges and universities where before few were allowed or ventured. Particularly with the unprecedented high levels of unemployment among young people, more of the young remain in education who before would have left to take a job. Schools, colleges and training centres have thus to accommodate a wide diversity of student talents, interests and backgrounds while attempting to discharge the onerous responsibility of giving each young person a preparation for adult life to the maximum of his or her capabilities.

The changing economic and social environment of education is the subject of a large part of this report. Prominence is given to the rapid structural change occurring in the economy. Technological developments multiply apace. The "information society" moves from cliché to reality as machines and networks that once were prohibitively expensive become household appliances. Work-time falls steadily while the length of retirement grows in most Member countries, raising the prospect of a new mixture of work and non-work and leisure throughout the economy. At the same time, these changes are accompanied by labour market difficulties with profound social consequences, most seriously the current high levels of unemployment that fall with particular severity upon certain groups – young people, those with few or no educational qualifications, older workers who most risk to remain among the long-term unemployed. More generally, there are troubling signs of the development of what might be termed the dual economy. The divide between those who are well rewarded and well integrated in the labour market, with secure high-skill jobs and careers, and those who do not enjoy these privileges may be getting wider and more difficult to traverse.

It is apparent in examining education's wider environment that the economic , the social and the cultural aspects of contemporary change are so interlocking that often they cannot meaningfully be separated. It is increasingly realised that economic performance is a function of the cultural values and social institutions in place in each country, education prominent among them. This takes on special significance as it comes also to be recognised that education's role in preparing and fostering non-cognitive traits, and values and attitudes more generally, may be just as critical a part of its impact upon the economy as its transmission of technical, cognitive knowledge and skills. Thus, education's role in equipping the populations of OECD countries for the economy and their working lives extends well beyond providing the "right" level and mix of knowledge and skills, important though this is. It has a far-reaching, if often intangible, effect upon such factors as productivity, entrepreneurial attitudes, saving and consumption habits, attitudes to innovation and to job satisfaction, industrial relations. But while most can agree that education is crucial in the transmission of values, it is much more difficult to agree how they should be integrated into schools and the curriculum. The issue is increasingly being confronted as the role played in education by communities and groups with their own particular values becomes greater.

In sum, education has to prepare people for a rapid and complex world of change and is itself a powerful vehicle that facilitates and guides this change. A central role for education and training derives from the fact that modern economies depend upon advanced knowledge and skills that are in a state of rapid evolution, hence generating the constant need for learning throughout the economically active population and a new balance between physical and human capital. Predictions of the precise impact of technological development upon job skills and employment levels differ widely but that these skills will undergo widespread change is generally recognised. The speed of technological change and the consequent obsolescence of knowledge, and the fact that most will change their jobs more than once during their working lives (and several times in many cases) clearly call for extensive recurrent education opportunities for professional training and retraining. The effects of rapid technical developments are felt in the organisation of work as well as in the skills required for different jobs. As the distinctions between scientists, engineers, technologists, technicians and craftsmen become more blurred, so does a new organisation of education and training need to be conceived.

This does not diminish the importance of basic education; indeed, it implies that each should achieve the soundest possible start which can be built upon throughout the rest of their lives. The fact and speed of change, however, place a premium upon the acquisition of more generic abilities, which can be classified broadly as "learning to learn", as well as the appetite and motivation for further learning. Technological developments appear increasingly to call for polyvalent skills and the ability to work in close co-operation with others that is not reflected in the "ethos" of much present educational provision, with its emphasis upon individual achievement and narrow specialisation. The tasks confronting the formal school system for children and young people are thus no less demanding than those of the education and training systems for adults.

With unemployment high and worrying signs of worsening segmentation and inequality in the labour market, education is vital too for the sizeable numbers who are only marginally attached to the workforce, who have insecure employment, or who are unemployed. Education cannot be expected to provide panaceas for their employment problems – it cannot create jobs. But it can improve the job chances of some that otherwise would be low or negligible by providing them with the competences required in the labour market. There are, however, significant limits to the ability of education generally to alter labour market chances as opposed to the position of the individual in the job queue, and this follows from its selective function. While education is intrinsically valuable and a well-developed education system has far-reaching benefits for economic performance, certificates and credentials also function importantly as selection mechanisms in the labour market, especially under present circumstances when there are severe shortages of jobs. The person with the credentials preferred by employers acquires critical competitive advantage in the job queue over those without them. It is for this reason that keeping everyone longer in education and training and ensuring that more leave with the requisite certificates, however good in itself, cannot be expected to "resolve" the labour market problems of those with the least qualifications since the function of the credentials is the distributive one of sorting and selecting for good jobs or poor, employment or unemployment. Indeed, as concluded in Chapter 4, those without qualifications, who are still drawn predominantly from the less privileged strata of society, may well be left further behind the more that others move ahead by taking advantage of the extensive opportunities for education and training now available. More than ever, therefore, the position of the least advantaged must be the object of serious policy concern. Otherwise, they risk being left far behind in an adult world that for some is high-skill and information-rich, but is not for others.

Specific groups and sections of the population – girls and women, migrants, cultural minorities, those in special regions, the handicapped – have become increasingly vocal in defining their own needs and in looking to rectify the educational disadvantage they suffer. For girls and women, this is most apparent in their serious under-representation in programmes and courses with greatest labour market value, particularly in technical branches, though this is indicative of the biases and inequities accumulated over the entire educational career. For cultural minorities, education systems have accommodated, indeed fostered, a greater degree of diversity than before. Yet, in designing and implementing special programmes for multi-culturalism, fundamental policy questions arise such as the point at which desirable diversity becomes unacceptable inequality of opportunity. This area also illustrates well the general question raised above: how far can new responsibilities and functions, such as the maintenance of different cultures, be fulfilled by schools already laden with high expectations and demands?

Education not only shapes and responds to social and economic change, but the very nature of education could well be transformed by them. One important aspect of this is the growing role of the community in education and the flourishing of non-formal learning opportunities, leading to the drawing of new boundaries between the "internal" world of education and its "external" environment. Even more radical realignments of the frontiers between education and its external environment are the potential consequences of the recent and unprecedented diffusion of the new information technologies in every sphere of society. It opens the possibility of significant change in the organisation of the classroom, the role and function of teachers, the management of learning, and the very location of education. The need to prepare rising generations to be functional in the world of rapid technological change requires curricular innovation and renewal, affecting teachers no less than students.

All of these changes have profound effects upon education and give rise to the new challenges and pressures it confronts. The report has emphasized the diversity of the student body and of their interests and needs and all sectors of education share the perturbing problem of coping with the differentiation that this leads to. In compulsory schooling, the need to give all – the gifted and the less gifted – equal chances to be educated to the maximum of their capabilities has led many Member countries to reform their organisation and adopt common educational structures at the secondary as well as primary school levels. But differentiation stubbornly persists and many countries realise how crucial are the qualitative factors that lie at the heart of the teaching-learning process as distinct from the organisational factors of educational structures. Much attention is now being given to the quality of school leadership and of teachers, to their qualifications and skills, and to the effective management and deployment of the available teaching resources.

At the post-compulsory level, the sheer breadth of talent and motivations of the student body is necessitating radical re-thinking of this sector in order that those who wish to continue their studies in higher education and those who enter the post-school world immediately can be equally catered for. Participation in both formal and non-formal programmes has grown and within the formal sector the most striking feature in most countries has been the increase of students in vocational lines. There still appears to be a shortage of technical programmes in many countries that prepare students for a level between first degree and basic vocational courses. Differentiation of status and "ethos" of the different branches continues to resist organisational reforms, so that a principal aim here is to bridge the gap between education and training and to reforge the links between the general and the vocational.

As with the post-compulsory sector, the diversity of the student body in higher education, particularly with the growing numbers of adults and non-traditional students pursuing a wide variety of programmes, is the central theme of Chapter 8. The conclusion emerges that the pressures for differentiation may well be leading to a growing polarisation of programmes and institutions into a relatively protected, perhaps selective, sector, on the one hand, and a more open, demand-oriented sector, on the other. This may be necessary in order that higher education continues to be at the forefront in providing the expertise and the advances in the frontiers of knowledge upon which modern societies depend. Protection of the research capacity of higher education, whose benefits tend always to be long-term, is essential and may well call for new institutional forms and links with external agencies. The evident risk of this polarisation, however, is that the "open" sector will be more vulnerable, the so-called soft subjects downgraded, and that the provision for non-traditional groups will no longer match that available for the more privileged, traditional student.

The contemporary developments, pressures and challenges facing education add up to the call for more education, not less; a growing demand that requires fresh thinking and clarity of purpose rather than simply "more of the same". In reaffirming the need for basic education of the highest quality, the importance of innovative and diverse initiatives in post-compulsory and higher education and the centrality of recurrent education in the changing social and economic environment of today, the arguments of the report imply that Member countries should move inexorably to become learning societies. At a time of financial constraints, this cannot be achieved without difficulties, though throughout the report, including Chapter 9, various avenues have been suggested for the more efficient use of resources and their redeployment. For example, educational buildings and facilities can be extended to broader community uses, new information technologies may permit greater efficiency in schools and colleges and in the use of teaching resources, and the preparation of teachers could be geared to allow greater flexibility and redeployment within the education system.

The resolution of these problems will form part of the general reappraisal by modern societies of the importance and scope of education today as new sources of revenue, new settings for education, new combinations of learning with other activities and new methods of teaching and learning are found and developed.

OECD SALES AGENTS
DÉPOSITAIRES DES PUBLICATIONS DE L'OCDE

ARGENTINA – ARGENTINE
Carlos Hirsch S.R.L., Florida 165, 4° Piso (Galería Guemes)
1333 BUENOS AIRES, Tel. 33.1787.2391 y 30.7122

AUSTRALIA – AUSTRALIE
Australia and New Zealand Book Company Pty, Ltd.,
10 Aquatic Drive, Frenchs Forest, N.S.W. 2086
P.O. Box 459, BROOKVALE, N.S.W. 2100. Tel. (02) 452.44.11

AUSTRIA – AUTRICHE
OECD Publications and Information Center
4 Simrockstrasse 5300 Bonn (Germany). Tel. (0228) 21.60.45
Local Agent/Agent local :
Gerold and Co., Graben 31, WIEN 1. Tel. 52.22.35

BELGIUM – BELGIQUE
Jean De Lannoy, Service Publications OCDE
avenue du Roi 202, B-1060 BRUXELLES. Tel. 02/538.51.69

CANADA
Renouf Publishing Company Limited,
Central Distribution Centre,
61 Sparks Street (Mall),
P.O.B. 1008 - Station B,
OTTAWA, Ont. K1P 5R1.
Tel. (613)238.8985-6
Toll Free: 1-800.267.4164
Librairie Renouf Limitée
980 rue Notre-Dame,
Lachine, P.Q. H8S 2B9,
Tel. (514) 634-7088.

DENMARK – DANEMARK
Munksgaard Export and Subscription Service
35, Nørre Søgade
DK 1370 KØBENHAVN K. Tel. +45.1.12.85.70

FINLAND – FINLANDE
Akateeminen Kirjakauppa
Keskuskatu 1, 00100 HELSINKI 10. Tel. 65.11.22

FRANCE
Bureau des Publications de l'OCDE,
2 rue André-Pascal, 75775 PARIS CEDEX 16. Tel. (1) 524.81.67
Principal correspondant :
13602 AIX-EN-PROVENCE : Librairie de l'Université.
Tel. 26.18.08

GERMANY – ALLEMAGNE
OECD Publications and Information Center
4 Simrockstrasse 5300 BONN (0228) 21.60.45

GREECE – GRÈCE
Librairie Kauffmann, 28 rue du Stade,
ATHÈNES 132. Tel. 322.21.60

HONG-KONG
Government Information Services,
Publications (Sales) Office,
Beaconsfield House, 4/F.,
Queen's Road Central

ICELAND – ISLANDE
Snaebjörn Jönsson and Co., h.f.,
Hafnarstraeti 4 and 9, P.O.B. 1131, REYKJAVIK.
Tel. 13133/14281/11936

INDIA – INDE
Oxford Book and Stationery Co. :
NEW DELHI-1, Scindia House. Tel. 45896
CALCUTTA 700016, 17 Park Street. Tel. 240832

INDONESIA – INDONÉSIE
PDIN-LIPI, P.O. Box 3065/JKT., JAKARTA, Tel. 583467

IRELAND – IRLANDE
TDC Publishers – Library Suppliers
12 North Frederick Street, DUBLIN 1 Tel. 744835-749677

ITALY – ITALIE
Libreria Commissionaria Sansoni :
Via Lamarmora 45, 50121 FIRENZE. Tel. 579751/584468
Via Bartolini 29, 20155 MILANO. Tel. 365083
Sub-depositari :
Ugo Tassi
Via A. Farnese 28, 00192 ROMA. Tel. 310590
Editrice e Libreria Herder,
Piazza Montecitorio 120, 00186 ROMA. Tel. 6794628
Costantino Ercolano, Via Generale Orsini 46, 80132 NAPOLI. Tel. 405210
Libreria Hoepli, Via Hoepli 5, 20121 MILANO. Tel. 865446
Libreria Scientifica, Dott. Lucio de Biasio "Aeiou"
Via Meravigli 16, 20123 MILANO Tel. 807679
Libreria Zanichelli
Piazza Galvani 1/A, 40124 Bologna Tel. 237389
Libreria Lattes, Via Garibaldi 3, 10122 TORINO. Tel. 519274
La diffusione delle edizioni OCSE è inoltre assicurata dalle migliori librerie nelle
città più importanti.

JAPAN – JAPON
OECD Publications and Information Center,
Landic Akasaka Bldg., 2-3-4 Akasaka,
Minato-ku, TOKYO 107 Tel. 586.2016

KOREA – CORÉE
Pan Korea Book Corporation,
P.O. Box n° 101 Kwangwhamun, SÉOUL. Tel. 72.7369

LEBANON – LIBAN
Documenta Scientifica/Redico,
Edison Building, Bliss Street, P.O. Box 5641, BEIRUT.
Tel. 354429 – 344425

MALAYSIA – MALAISIE
University of Malaya Co-operative Bookshop Ltd.
P.O. Box 1127, Jalan Pantai Baru
KUALA LUMPUR. Tel. 577701/577072

THE NETHERLANDS – PAYS-BAS
Staatsuitgeverij, Verzendboekhandel,
Chr. Plantijnstraat 1 Postbus 20014
2500 EA S-GRAVENHAGE. Tel. nr. 070.789911
Voor bestellingen: Tel. 070.789208

NEW ZEALAND – NOUVELLE-ZÉLANDE
Publications Section,
Government Printing Office Bookshops:
AUCKLAND: Retail Bookshop: 25 Rutland Street,
Mail Orders: 85 Beach Road, Private Bag C.P.O.
HAMILTON: Retail: Ward Street,
Mail Orders, P.O. Box 857
WELLINGTON: Retail: Mulgrave Street (Head Office),
Cubacade World Trade Centre
Mail Orders: Private Bag
CHRISTCHURCH: Retail: 159 Hereford Street,
Mail Orders: Private Bag
DUNEDIN: Retail: Princes Street
Mail Order: P.O. Box 1104

NORWAY – NORVÈGE
J.G. TANUM A/S
P.O. Box 1177 Sentrum OSLO 1. Tel. (02) 80.12.60

PAKISTAN
Mirza Book Agency, 65 Shahrah Quaid-E-Azam, LAHORE 3.
Tel. 66839

PORTUGAL
Livraria Portugal, Rua do Carmo 70-74,
1117 LISBOA CODEX. Tel. 360582/3

SINGAPORE – SINGAPOUR
Information Publications Pte Ltd,
Pei-Fu Industrial Building,
24 New Industrial Road N° 02-06
SINGAPORE 1953, Tel. 2831786, 2831798

SPAIN – ESPAGNE
Mundi-Prensa Libros, S.A.
Castelló 37, Apartado 1223, MADRID-28001, Tel. 275.46.55
Libreria Bosch, Ronda Universidad 11, BARCELONA 7.
Tel. 317.53.08, 317.53.58

SWEDEN – SUÈDE
AB CE Fritzes Kungl Hovbokhandel,
Box 16 356, S 103 27 STH, Regeringsgatan 12,
DS STOCKHOLM. Tel. 08/23.89.00
Subscription Agency/Abonnements:
Wennergren-Williams AB,
Box 30004, S104 25 STOCKHOLM.
Tel. 08/54.12.00

SWITZERLAND – SUISSE
OECD Publications and Information Center
4 Simrockstrasse 5300 BONN (Germany). Tel. (0228) 21.60.45
Local Agents/Agents locaux
Librairie Payot, 6 rue Grenus, 1211 GENÈVE 11. Tel. 022.31.89.50

TAIWAN – FORMOSE
Good Faith Worldwide Int'l Co., Ltd.
9th floor, No. 118, Sec. 2,
Chung Hsiao E. Road
TAIPEI. Tel. 391.7396/391.7397

THAILAND – THAILANDE
Suksit Siam Co., Ltd., 1715 Rama IV Rd,
Samyan, BANGKOK 5. Tel. 2511630

TURKEY – TURQUIE
Kültur Yayinlari Is-Türk Ltd. Sti.
Atatürk Bulvari No : 191/Kat. 21
Kavaklidere/ANKARA. Tel. 17 02 66
Dolmabahce Cad. No : 29
BESIKTAS/ISTANBUL. Tel. 60 71 88

UNITED KINGDOM – ROYAUME-UNI
H.M. Stationery Office,
P.O.B. 276, LONDON SW8 5DT.
(postal orders only)
Telephone orders: (01) 622.3316, or
49 High Holborn, LONDON WC1V 6 HB (personal callers)
Branches at: EDINBURGH, BIRMINGHAM, BRISTOL,
MANCHESTER, BELFAST.

UNITED STATES OF AMERICA – ÉTATS-UNIS
OECD Publications and Information Center, Suite 1207,
1750 Pennsylvania Ave., N.W. WASHINGTON, D.C.20006 – 4582
Tel. (202) 724.1857

VENEZUELA
Libreria del Este, Avda. F. Miranda 52, Edificio Galipan,
CARACAS 106. Tel. 32.23.01/33.26.04/31.58.38

YUGOSLAVIA – YOUGOSLAVIE
Jugoslovenska Knjiga, Knez Mihajlova 2, P.O.B. 36, BEOGRAD.
Tel. 621.992

Les commandes provenant de pays où l'OCDE n'a pas encore désigné de dépositaire peuvent être adressées à :
OCDE, Bureau des Publications, 2, rue André-Pascal, 75775 PARIS CEDEX 16.

Orders and inquiries from countries where sales agents have not yet been appointed may be sent to:
OECD, Publications Office, 2, rue André-Pascal, 75775 PARIS CEDEX 16.

OECD PUBLICATIONS, 2, rue André-Pascal, 75775 PARIS CEDEX 16 - No. 43235 1985
PRINTED IN FRANCE
(91 85 02 1) ISBN 92-64-12739-9